Secure Searchable Encryption and Data Management

Secure Searchable Encryption and Data Management

Brij B. Gupta
Mamta

CRC Press
Taylor & Francis Group
Boca Raton London New York

CRC Press is an imprint of the
Taylor & Francis Group, an **informa** business

First Edition published 2021
by CRC Press
6000 Broken Sound Parkway NW, Suite 300, Boca Raton, FL 33487-2742

and by CRC Press
2 Park Square, Milton Park, Abingdon, Oxon, OX14 4RN

© 2021 Taylor & Francis Group, LLC

CRC Press is an imprint of Taylor & Francis Group, LLC

ISBN: 978-0-367-61967-1 (hbk)
ISBN: 978-0-367-70673-9 (pbk)
ISBN: 978-1-003-10731-6 (ebk)

Typeset in Sabon
by KnowledgeWorks Global Ltd.

Dedicated to my parents and family for their constant support during the course of this book

— *Brij B. Gupta*

Dedicated to my parents, son, beloved husband and my mentor for their motivation throughout the journey of completion of this book.

— *Mamta*

Contents

Preface

WITH THE ADVENT OF THE IT REVOLUTION, the volume of data produced has increased exponentially and is still showing an upward trend. This data may be abundant and enormous but it's a precious resource and should be managed properly. Cloud technology plays an important role in data management. Storing data in the cloud rather than on local storage has many benefits, but apart from these benefits there are privacy concerns in storing sensitive data over third-party servers; these concerns can be addressed by storing data in an encrypted form. However, while encryption solves the problem of privacy it engenders other serious issues, including the infeasibility of the fundamental search operation and a reduction in flexibility when sharing the data with other users, amongst others. The concept of searchable encryption addresses these issues. This book covers the origin and essential mathematical background required to understand and develop searchable encryption schemes. It includes chapters that provide an extensive classification of searchable encryption schemes in both symmetric-key and public-key settings. These chapters describe the searchable encryption schemes under each category based on their features, security and efficiency. Further, the authors have performed a comparative study of searchable encryption schemes under each category by computing the computational as well as the storage costs. Different tools, libraries and datasets used for the development of searchable encryption schemes are also covered. The book also discusses inter-domain applications of searchable encryption schemes. Finally, it casts light upon open research challenges and future research directions to guide researchers and practitioners for further evolution of this field.

This book is designed for readers with an interest in the field of security, particularly those who want to work on ensuring confidentiality while performing operations on encrypted data. This includes researchers who are exploring the pros and cons associated with the technology and developers and security professionals who are focusing on developing secure searchable encryption schemes that can have applications in variety of areas.

Specifically, this book contains seven chapters, a detailed overview of the topics covered by each chapter is summarized as follows:

Chapter 1: Introduction to number theory and abstract algebra – This chapter introduces the fundamentals of number theory and abstract algebra as preliminary knowledge required to understand any cryptographic algorithm.

Chapter 2: Introduction to cryptography – This chapter covers the basic concepts related to cryptography. It briefly discusses both traditional and the modern cryptography along with the journey from traditional to modern cryptography. It describes the cryptographic principles and the key terms in detail so as to build a strong background.

Chapter 3: Searchable encryption and data management – This chapter formally introduces the concept of searchable encryption as a data management technique. It explains the need of such a technique and how this technique can be used to solve the problem of confidentiality and efficient retrieval of desired information out of the encrypted data without breaching the confidentiality. This chapter discusses the broad categories of searchable encryption depending upon the underlying encryption technique. It also explains which underlying encryption technique can provide more benefits to its users in different scenarios.

Chapter 4: Introduction to provable security and its application in searchable encryption – This chapter introduces the concept of provable security and its application in developing a secure searchable encryption. This chapter gives the basic security definitions used in searchable encryption and also explains the different security models that can be employed to prove security for a searchable encryption scheme. Moreover, this chapter provides an introduction to cryptographic assumptions used in provable security and cites the commonly used assumptions in searchable encryption.

Chapter 5: Searchable encryption in a public-key setting – This chapter explains in detail the concept of searchable encryption in a public-key setting. It provides the general structure of the searchable encryption scheme in an asymmetric-key setting. Further, this chapter compares the existing schemes in literature in this setting and also discusses possible scope for improvement.

Chapter 6: Design and development tools and inter-domain applications – This chapter discusses different open-source tools for the design and development of secure searchable encryption schemes. Further, it discusses the inter-domain application of searchable encryption and how this technique plays an important role in different domains.

Chapter 7: Searchable encryption applications, challenges and future research directions – This chapter highlights the open challenges associated with searchable encryption and provides an insight of the future research directions in the field.

Acknowledgements

First of all, we would like to pay our gratitude to God by bowing our heads for lavishing us with continuous blessings and enthusiasm for completing this book. Writing a book is not a work of an individual, but it is the outcome of the incessant support of our loved ones. This book is the result of inestimable hard work, continuous efforts and the assistance of loved ones. Therefore, we would like to express our gratefulness to everyone linked to this book, either directly or indirectly, for their exquisite cooperation and creative ideas for ameliorating the quality of this book. Along with this feeling, we would like to thank the CRC Press/Taylor & Francis Group team and staff members for their assistance and persistent support. We are grateful, from the bottom of our hearts, to our family members for their absolute love and uncountable prayers. This experience is both internally challenging and rewarding. Therefore, again, special thanks to all who helped us in making this happen.

Author bio

Brij B. Gupta received his PhD degree from the Indian Institute of Technology in Roorkee, India, in the area of Information and Cyber Security. He has published more than 250 research papers in international journals and conferences of high repute. He has visited several countries, for example Canada, Japan, USA, UK, Malaysia, Australia, Thailand, China, Hong Kong, Italy, Spain, etc., to present his research work. His biography was selected and published in the 30th Edition of *Marquis Who's Who in the World*, 2012. Dr. Gupta also received the Young Faculty Research Fellowship award from the Ministry of Electronics and Information Technology, Government of India, in 2018. He also works as a principal investigator of various R&D projects. He is serving/has served as associate editor of *IEEE Access*, IEEE TII, FGCS, IJICS, IJCSE, ACM TOIT, ASOC, etc. At present, Dr. Gupta works as an assistant professor in the Department of Computer Engineering at the National Institute of Technology, Kurukshetra, India. His research interests include information security, cyber security, mobile security, cloud computing, web security, intrusion detection and phishing.

Mamta is currently pursuing her PhD in Applied Cryptography under the Supervision of Dr. Brij B. Gupta in the Department of Computer Engineering at the National Institute of Technology (NIT), Kurukshetra, India. She has received her M.Tech. from the Department of Computer Engineering at the National Institute of Technology, Kurukshetra, India. She has received her B.Tech. degree in Computer Engineering from the University Institute of Engineering and Technology, Kurukshetra University. Her research interests include number theory and cryptography, searchable encryption, information security and cloud computing. She has published various research articles with various reputed publishers, like IEEE, Springer, Wiley, and IGI Global.

Chapter 1

Introduction to number theory and abstract algebra

NUMBER THEORY AND ABSTRACT ALGEBRA plays an important role in the development of cryptosystems. Their basic knowledge acts as a key ingredient to the fields like cryptography and coding theory. Therefore, in this chapter, we will give a detailed overview of these basic concepts to build a strong foundation before diving deep into the field of searchable encryption and data management. This chapter is divided two parts, the first part covers the concepts related to number theory and the second part covers the basic concepts of abstract algebra.

1.1 NUMBER THEORY

Number theory is an interesting facet of mathematics that has attracted everyone from professional mathematicians to amateurs with its captivating concepts. Number theory concepts and theorems are natural and make sense even to a layman. However, proving them essentially requires both the basic knowledge and strong background we expect from a graduate in Computer Engineering. In this section, we will cover all the necessary concepts of number theory needed for the development of searchable encryption schemes along with their detailed proofs [1].

1.1.1 Divisibility

Divisibility is the fundamental concept of number theory. Consider a set of integers, $Z = \{..., -1, 0, 1, ...\}$, we say b divides a, $(b \mid a)$, if $a = k \cdot b$, where $a, b, k \in Z$ [2]. Alternatively, one can also say that a is divisible by b, or a is a multiple of b, or b is a factor/divisor of a. The trivial cases include: i) $\forall b \in Z$, $b \mid 0$, which denotes that every number divides 0, and ii) $\forall a \in Z$, $1 \mid a$, which denotes that 1 divides every number.

1.1.1.1 Divisibility properties

The following are key properties of divisibility, which can be easily verified with the definition of divisibility:

- If $a|b$ and $b|c$ then $a|c$
- If $a|b$ then $a|bc$, $\forall c \in Z$
- If $a|b$ and $c|d$ then $ac|bd$
- If m: non-zero integer, then $a|b$ iff $ma|mb$
- If $a|x$ and $a|y$ then $a|cx+dy$, where $c,d \in Z$
- If d: non-zero integer such that $d|a$ and $a \neq 0$ then $|d| \leq |a|$
- $a|b$ and $b|a$ iff $a = \pm b$
- If $a|b$ and $a|c$ then $a|b \pm c$

If $a|b$, $b = k_1 \cdot a$ and $b|c$, $c = k_2 \cdot b = k_2 \cdot (k_1 \cdot a) = k \cdot a$, where $k = k_1 \cdot k_2 \in Z$. Hence, by definition, $a|c$. Similarly, other properties can also be proved using the basic algebraic properties and the definition of divisibility and are left as an exercise due to constraints on the book length.

An integer may not be completely divisible by another; in that case there will be a quotient (q) and a remainder (r). The division theorem states this fact as, for any integer a and a positive integer n, $\exists$ a unique integer q and r: $0 \leq r < n$ and $a = q \cdot n + r$. If a number is completely divisible then $r = 0$; otherwise, $r \in [1, n-1]$.

1.1.2 Prime numbers

For any integer, $x > 1$, there exists at least two positive divisors, x and 1, which are called trivial divisors for that number. A number is said to be prime if there exists no non-trivial divisor for it. If there exists at least one non-trivial divisor, then that number is called a composite number [2].

Theorem 1: There are infinite number of primes.

Proof: The proof is by contradiction. Let there are finite number of primes: $(2,3,\ldots\ldots,p_k)$ and p_k is the largest prime. Construct another number m: product of all primes +1.

Observation: None of the primes can divide m (leaves remainder 1). So, m is divisible by 1 and itself, hence m must be another prime number. In this way one can construct an infinite number of primes.

1.1.2.1 Fundamental theorem of arithmetic

The fundamental theorem of arithmetic states that every positive integer can be represented uniquely as the product of primes, i.e. $n = p_1^{e_1} \cdot p_2^{e_2} \cdots\cdots p_m^{e_m}$, where

$p_1 < p_2 < \cdots\cdots < p_m$ and all are distinct [3]. For example: $100 = 2 \cdot 2 \cdot 5 \cdot 5 = 2^2 \cdot 5^2$; $81 = 3^4$.

The proof is by contradiction. Let there are two different prime factorizations of n:

- $n = p_1^{e_1} \cdot p_2^{e_2} \cdots\cdots p_m^{e_m}$
- $n = q_1^{d_1} \cdot q_2^{d_2} \cdots\cdots q_r^{d_r}$

Therefore, $p_1^{e_1} \cdot p_2^{e_2} \cdots\cdots p_m^{e_m} = q_1^{d_1} \cdot q_2^{d_2} \cdots\cdots q_r^{d_r}$. Now, we have to prove $p_1 = q_1$ and $e_1 = d_1$ provided $p_1 = q_1$.

- If $p_1 \neq q_1$, then p_1 can't divide any of the primes $q_1,\ldots\ldots q_r \cdot p_1$ is relatively prime to all $q_1,\ldots\ldots q_r$, then p_1 cannot divide n (because $n = q_1^{d_1} \cdot q_2^{d_2} \cdots\cdots q_r^{d_r}$). But this is not true. Hence $p_1 = q_1$
- Assume $e_1 < d_1$ then $d_1 = e_1 + h, h > 0$

$$p_1^{e_1} \cdot p_2^{e_2} \cdots\cdots p_m^{e_m} = q_1^{d_1} \cdot q_2^{d_2} \cdots\cdots q_r^{d_r}$$

$$p_1^{e_1} \cdot p_2^{e_2} \cdots\cdots p_m^{e_m} = q_1^{e_1+h} \cdot q_2^{d_2} \cdots\cdots q_r^{d_r}$$

$$p_2^{e_2} \cdots\cdots p_m^{e_m} = q_1^{h} \cdot q_2^{d_2} \cdots\cdots q_r^{d_r}$$

From the above equation we can observe that RHS is divisible by q_1 while the LHS is not, which is impossible. Hence $e_1 = d_1$

1.1.2.2 Prime number properties

Following are the key properties of the prime numbers:

- If a prime number p divides ab then either $p|a$ or $p|b$.
- If $m|a$ and $n|a$, and if m and n has no divisor greater than 1 in common (i.e. m and n are relatively prime) then $mn|a$.
- If $p^{\alpha}\|n$, then $p^{\beta}\|n$ for some $0 \leq \beta \leq \alpha$.

Let $n = p_1^{\alpha_1} \cdot p_2^{\alpha_2} \cdots. p_r^{\alpha_r}$, the total number of divisors of n is the product of the number of possibilities for each prime power, i.e. $(\alpha_1 + 1)(\alpha_2 + 1)\ldots\ldots(\alpha_r + 1)$

1.1.3 Greatest common divisor (GCD)

The greatest common divisor of two numbers a and b, $gcd(a, b)$, is the largest integer d that divides both a and b.

$$gcd(a, b) = max\{d : d|a \ and \ d|b\}$$

If we have prime factorization of a and b then $gcd(a, b)$ can be easily written as follows:

- Given $a = p_1^{\alpha_1} \cdot p_2^{\alpha_2} \cdot \ldots \cdot p_k^{\alpha_k}$ and $b = p_1^{\beta_1} \cdot p_2^{\beta_2} \cdot \ldots \cdot p_k^{\beta_k}$.
- Take all the primes which occur in both factorizations raised to the minimum of two exponents.
- $gcd(a, b) = p_1^{min(\alpha_1, \beta_1)} \ldots \ldots p_k^{min(\alpha_k, \beta_k)}$.

Relatively prime numbers: The integers $a_1, a_2, \ldots \ldots, a_k$ are pairwise relatively prime if $gcd(a_i, a_j) = 1, \forall\ 1 \le i, j \le k$.

1.1.3.1 Euclid's theorem

Let $b, c > 0$ and $c \nmid b$; using the division theorem we can obtain the following equations:

$$b = cq_1 + r_1; \ 0 < r_1 < c \tag{1.1}$$

$$c = r_1 q_2 + r_2; \ 0 < r_2 < r_1 \tag{1.2}$$

$$r_1 = r_2 q_3 + r_3; \ 0 < r_3 < r_2 \tag{1.3}$$

$$r_{j-2} = r_{j-1} q_j + r_j; \ 0 < r_j < r_{j-1} \tag{1.4}$$

$$r_{j-1} = r_j q_{j+1} + 0 \tag{1.5}$$

Then, $gcd(b, c) = r_j$, which represents the last non-zero remainder in the above set of equations.

In the above algorithm, we see that the remainder decreases until it becomes 0. Further, the remainders do not only decrease but they decrease rather rapidly. In every two steps the size of the remainder becomes at least half, i.e. $r_{j+2} < \frac{1}{2} r_j$.

Proof: If $r_{j+1} \le \frac{1}{2} r_j$ then $r_{j+2} < r_{j+1} \le \frac{1}{2} r_j$. Suppose $r_{j+1} > \frac{1}{2} r_j$ then $r_j = 1 \cdot r_{j+1} + r_{j+2}$.

Alternatively, we can write, $r_{j+2} = r_j - r_{j+1}$. If $r_{j+1} > \frac{1}{2} r_j$, then $r_{j+2} < \frac{1}{2} r_j$.

1.1.3.2 Extended Euclidean algorithm

Let $d = gcd(a, b)$. Then there exists integers u and v such that $d = ua + vb$, i.e. GCD of two numbers can be expressed as a linear combination of the numbers with integer coefficient.

For example: $gcd(560, 1547)$
First, apply Euclid's theorem to find the gcd as follows:

1. $1547 = 2 \cdot 560 + 427$
2. $560 = 1 \cdot 427 + 133$
3. $427 = 3 \cdot 133 + 28$
4. $133 = 4 \cdot 28 + 21$
5. $28 = 1 \cdot 21 + 7$

Now, backtrack from the last equations and recursively put values until we get the original numbers:

$$7 = 28 - 1 \cdot (21)$$
$$= 28 - 1 \cdot (133 - 4 \cdot 28)$$
$$= 28 - 133 + 4 \cdot (28)$$
$$= 5 \cdot (28) - 133$$
$$= 5 \cdot (427 - 3 \cdot (133)) - 133$$
$$= 5 \cdot 427 - 16 \cdot 133$$
$$= 5 \cdot 427 - 16(560 - 427)$$
$$= 21 \cdot 427 - 16 \cdot 560$$
$$= 21(1547 - 2 \cdot 560) - 16 \cdot 560$$
$$= 21 \cdot 1547 + (-58) \cdot 560$$

The extended Euclid algorithm has application in finding the multiplicative inverse.

1.1.4 Congruence

If an integer m divides the difference $a - b$, then we say a is congruent to $b \bmod m$, i.e. $a \equiv b \bmod m$ iff $m | a - b$ [2], [3].

1.1.4.1 Congruence relation properties

The following are the key properties of congruence:

- If $a \equiv b (mod m)$ and $c \equiv d (mod m)$, then $a \pm c \equiv (b \pm d) mod m$ and $ac \equiv bd mod m$.
- If $a \equiv b (mod m)$ and $b \equiv c (mod m)$, then $a \equiv c (mod m)$.
- If $a \equiv b (mod m)$, $b \equiv a (mod m)$ and $a - b \equiv 0 (mod m)$ are equivalent.
- If $a \equiv b (mod m)$ and $d | m$, $d > 0$ then $a \equiv b (mod d)$.
- If $a \equiv b (mod m)$ then $ac \equiv bc (mod mc)$ for $c > 0$.

- If $a \equiv b \bmod m$, $a \equiv b \bmod n$ and m, n are relatively prime then $a \equiv b \bmod mn$.
- Congruence modulo n is an equivalence relation on Z.
  - Reflexive: $a \equiv a \bmod n \; \forall a \in Z$
  - Symmetry: If $a \equiv b \bmod n$ then $b \equiv a \bmod n$
  - Transitive: If $a \equiv b \bmod n$ and $b \equiv c \bmod n$ then $a \equiv c \bmod n$

The proof of these properties can be done with the help of the definition of congruence and basic integer algebra. We will provide the proof of the first property and others can also be proven in the same manner as follows: If $a \equiv b(\bmod m)$ then by the congruence definition and divisibility theorem, we can write: $a - b = s \cdot m$ and $c - d = t \cdot m$, where $s, t \in Z$; $a + c = (s + t)m + (b + d)$, $s + t \in$. Hence, $a \pm c \equiv (b \pm d) \bmod m$. Similarly, $ac = (st)m + (bd)$, $st \in Z$. Hence, $ac \equiv bd \bmod m$.

1.1.4.1.1 Congruence (residue) classes modulo m

If $x \equiv y(\bmod m)$, then y is called a residue when we divide x by m. A set $x_1, x_2, \cdots, x_m$ is called a complete residue system modulo m, if $\forall y \in Z, \exists$ a unique x_j: $y \equiv x_j(\bmod m)$.

For fixed integer a and $m > 0$, the set of all integers, x, satisfying $x \equiv a(\bmod m)$ forms an arithmetic progression (AP), $\{......a - 2m, a - m, a + m, a + 2m......\}$ and this set is called a residue class or congruence class modulo m. For example: equivalence classes of 0 and 1 for congruence modulo 4 are: $[0]_4 = \{......-8, -4, 0, 4, 8......\}$ and $[1]_4 = \{......-9, -5, 1, 5, 9......\}$.

1.1.4.2 Reduced residue system modulo m

A reduced residue system modulo m is a set of integers, r_i: $(r_i, m) = 1$, $r_i \not\equiv r_j(\bmod m)$ if $i \neq j$ and such that every integer relatively prime to m is congruent modulo m to some member r_i of the set. To get the reduced residue from the complete residue system, delete all members y for which $(y, m) \neq 1$.

1.1.4.3 Inverse modulo m

If $\gcd(a, m) = 1$ or $(a, m) = 1$ then there is an x: $ax \equiv 1 \bmod m$ and x is called the multiplicative inverse of $a \bmod m$.

> *Proof*: By the extended Euclidean algorithm: $\gcd(a, m) = ax + my = 1 \Rightarrow m \mid ax - 1 \Rightarrow ax \equiv 1 \bmod$. Conversely, if $ax \equiv 1 \bmod m \Rightarrow m \mid ax - 1$, then $\exists y$: $ax + my = 1$.

Therefore, if $m > 1$ and $\gcd(a, m) = 1$, then inverse of $a \bmod m$ exists and is equal to x in the following representation of $\gcd(a, m)$: $ax + my = 1$.

1.1.4.4 Euler's phi function (totient function)

The number of elements in a reduced residue system modulo m is denoted by $\varphi(m)$ called Euler's phi function or the totient function or indicator function. It is used for counting relatively prime numbers. For example: how many positive numbers less than 20 are relatively prime to 20? The answer is: 1, 3, 7, 9, 11, 13, 17, 19.

To find a formula for $\varphi(n)$:

- Make a table for $\varphi(n)$ for $n = 1, 2, \ldots\ldots, 15$

n	1	2	3	4	5	6	7	8	9	10	11	12	13	14	15
$\varphi(n)$	1	1	2	2	4	2	6	4	6	4	10	4	12	6	8

- If p is prime check in the table what is $\varphi(p)$?
- $\varphi(p) = p - 1$
- If p is a prime number and k is a whole number
  - The numbers less than (or equal to) p^k that are not relatively prime to p^k would surely be multiples of p, i.e. $p, 2p, \ldots\ldots, p^{k-1}p$
  - So there are p^{k-1} out of p^k which are not relatively prime
  - $\varphi(p^k) = p^k - p^{k-1}$

1.1.4.5 Fermat's theorem

Let p denotes a prime. If $p \nmid a$ then $a^{p-1} \equiv 1 \bmod p$

Proof: If $p \nmid a \Rightarrow (a, p) = 1 \Rightarrow a^{\varphi(p)} \equiv 1 \bmod p$ by the Euler's generalization of Fermat's theorem. $\varphi(p)$ denotes the number of integers relatively prime to p, which are $p - 1$. Hence, $a^{p-1} \equiv 1 \bmod p$.

1.1.4.6 Euler's generalization of Fermat's theorem

If $(a, m) = 1$, then $a^{\varphi(m)} \equiv 1 \bmod m$.

Proof: Let $r_1, r_2, \cdots, r_{\varphi(m)}$ be a reduced residue system modulo m. Then $ar_1, ar_2, \cdots, ar_{\varphi(m)}$ is also a reduced residue system modulo m, since $(a, m) = 1$ and $(r_i, m) = 1$, which implies $(ar_i, m) = 1$. Therefore, corresponding to each r_i, there is one and only one ar_j such that $ar_j \equiv r_i (\bmod m)$. Multiply all such $\varphi(m)$ relations: $\prod_{j=1}^{\varphi(m)} ar_j \equiv \prod_{i=1}^{\varphi(m)} r_i (\bmod m) = a^{\varphi(m)} \equiv 1 \bmod m$.

1.1.5 Congruence solutions

Let $m_1, m_2, \ldots\ldots m_r$ be pairwise relatively prime positive integers. We want to find the solution of the following system: $x \equiv a_1 \bmod m_1$, $x \equiv a_2 \bmod m_2$, ..., $x \equiv a_r \bmod m_r$ One method to find the solution of such equations is by the Chinese remainder theorem (CRT).

The CRT theorem states that the solution of such system exists if $(m_i, m_j) = 1, \forall i \neq j$.

Proof: Let $m = m_1 \cdot m_2 \cdot \ldots \cdot m_r$, then $\left(\dfrac{m}{m_j}, m_j \right) = 1$. Let $R(m_j)$ represents the reduced residue modulo m, which contains set of all elements relatively prime to m_j. Therefore, $\forall a \in R(m_j), \exists x \in R(m_j): ax \equiv 1 mod m_j$, which implies, $\exists b_j \in R(m_j): \dfrac{m}{m_j} \cdot b_j \equiv 1 mod m_j$. Let x_0 be the one solution, then

$$x_0 = \sum_{j=1}^{r} \left(\frac{m}{m_j} \right) \cdot b_j \cdot a_j mod \; m_j \; \text{because} \left(\frac{m}{m_j} \right) \cdot b_j \cdot a_j \equiv a_j mod m_j.$$

1.1.6 Quadratic residues

If p is an odd prime and a is an integer relatively prime to p then is "a" a perfect square modulo p? Finding quadratic residues provides the answer to this question. If m is a positive integer, we say integer "a" is a quadratic residue of m if $gcd(a, m) = 1$ and the congruence $x^2 \equiv a mod m$ has a solution. If $x^2 \equiv a mod m$ has no solution then "a" is a quadratic non-residue of m [2], [3].

Example: Determine which integers are quadratic residues of 11.
- Step 1: Since $m = 11$ is a prime number then $\{1, 2, \ldots 10\}$ are relatively prime to m.
- Step 2: Compute the squares of integers $\{1, 2, \ldots 10\}$: $1^2 \equiv 10^2 \equiv 1 mod 11$, $2^2 \equiv 9^2 \equiv 4 mod 11, 3^2 \equiv 8^2 \equiv 9 mod 11, 4^2 \equiv 7^2 \equiv 5 mod 11, 5^2 \equiv 6^2 \equiv 3 mod 11$.
- Quadratic residues: 1, 3, 4, 5, 9, Quadratic non-residues: 2, 6, 7, 8, 10.

Conclusion: Given any fixed positive integer m, it is possible to determine the quadratic residue by simply listing the positive integers less than and prime to m, squaring them and reducing $mod m$.

Lemma: If p is an odd prime and a is an integer relatively prime to p then the congruence $x^2 \equiv a mod m$ has either no solution or exactly two incongruent solutions modulo p.

Proof: If $x^2 \equiv a mod p$ has a solution, say $x = x_0$, then we can easily demonstrate that $x = -x_0$ is the second incongruent solution because $(-x_0)^2 = x_0^2 \equiv a mod p$. *Note*: $x_0 \not\equiv -x_0 mod p$ $(2x_0 \equiv 0 mod p$, which is impossible because $p | x_0)$.

Now we have to show that there are no more than two incongruent solutions. Assume $x = x_0$ and $x = x_1$ are both solutions of $x^2 \equiv a mod p$. $x_0^2 \equiv a mod p$ and $x_1^2 \equiv a mod p$ then $x_0^2 - x_1^2 \equiv 0 mod p$. $(x_0 + x_1)(x_0 - x_1) \equiv 0 mod p$ i.e. $p | (x_0 + x_1)$ or $p | (x_0 - x_1)$. $x_1 \equiv -x_0 mod p$ or $x_1 \equiv x_0 mod p$.

Theorem: If p is an odd prime then there are exactly $\dfrac{p-1}{2}$ quadratic residues of p and $\dfrac{p-1}{2}$ quadratic non-residues of p.

Proof: Consider all the squares of integers $\{1, 2, \dots p-1\}$. We know $x^2 \equiv (p-x)^2 \equiv a \bmod p$. Let $1 < b < p-1$. $(p-b)^2 \equiv b^2 \bmod p$.

$$1^2, 2^2, \dots, \left(\frac{p-1}{2}\right)^2 \equiv \left(\frac{p+1}{2}\right)^2, \dots, (p-2)^2, (p-1)^2 \tag{1.6}$$

Since $1^2 \equiv (p-1)^2 \bmod p$ and similarly the same relation can be set among other elements of equation (1.6). Therefore, $1^2, 2^2, \dots, \left(\frac{p-1}{2}\right)^2$ are all distinct.

1.1.6.1 Euler's criterion

Euler's criterion tells us precisely when an integer a is a quadratic residue modulo an odd prime p. Let p be odd prime and $gcd(a, p) = 1$. Then a is a quadratic residue modulo p if and only if $a^{\frac{p-1}{2}} \equiv 1 \bmod p$

Proof: Let a be the quadratic residue then $x^2 \equiv a \bmod p$. $(x^2)^{\frac{p-1}{2}} \equiv a^{\frac{p-1}{2}} \bmod p$. $x^{p-1} \equiv a^{\frac{p-1}{2}} \bmod p$. By Fermat's little theorem, $x^{p-1} \equiv 1 \bmod p$, therefore, $a^{\frac{p-1}{2}} \equiv 1 \bmod p$.

Conversely: Given $a^{\frac{p-1}{2}} \equiv 1 \bmod p$. To prove: "$a$" is a quadratic residue modulo an odd prime p.

Proof: We know that there exists a primitive root g *modulo* p, such that any integer in $\mathbb{Z}_p$ can be expressed as $g^i \bmod p$, $1 \le i \le p-1$ and $g^m \equiv 1 \bmod p$ holds only when $p-1 | m$ ($m = 0$ or $p-1$). For some $1 \le i \le p-1$ we have

$a \equiv g^i \bmod p$. $g^{i\left(\frac{p-1}{2}\right)} \equiv a^{\frac{p-1}{2}} \equiv 1 \bmod p$ (Given). By the property of primitive root $p-1 | i\left(\frac{p-1}{2}\right)$; therefore, i must be even say, $i = 2j$ which implies $a \equiv g^{2j} \bmod p$, $a \equiv (g^j)^2 \bmod p$. Hence, a is a quadratic residue modulo an odd prime p.

1.1.7 Legendre symbol

It is a convenient notation to indicate whether an integer a is a quadratic residue modulo an odd prime p. Legendre symbol of $a \bmod p$ is denoted as $\left(\dfrac{a}{p}\right)$. Formally, it is defined as:

$$\left(\frac{a}{p}\right) = \begin{cases} 1, & \text{if } a \text{ is a } non-zero \text{ quadratic residue modulo p} \\ -1, & \text{if } a \text{ is a } non-zero \text{ quadratic non-residue modulo p} \\ 0, & \text{if } p | a \end{cases} \tag{1.7}$$

Example: $\left(\dfrac{2}{7}\right) = 1, \left(\dfrac{2}{5}\right) = -1, \left(\dfrac{12}{5}\right) = -1, \left(\dfrac{101}{97}\right) = 1, \left(\dfrac{97}{101}\right) = 1.$

If p divide a with remainder, i.e. $a = qp + r$ then $\left(\dfrac{a}{p}\right) = \left(\dfrac{r}{p}\right)$. By Euler's criterion, $a^{\frac{p-1}{2}} \equiv \left(\dfrac{a}{p}\right) mod\, p$.

1.1.7.1 Law of quadratic reciprocity

The law of quadratic reciprocity relates the two Legendre symbols $\left(\dfrac{p}{q}\right)$ and $\left(\dfrac{q}{p}\right)$ where p and q are odd primes:

$$\left(\frac{p}{q}\right)\left(\frac{q}{p}\right) = (-1)^{\left(\frac{p-1}{2}\right)\left(\frac{q-1}{2}\right)} \tag{1.8}$$

Where $\dfrac{p-1}{2}$ is even when $p \equiv 1(mod\,4)$ and odd when $p \equiv 3(mod\,4)$. Consequently, $\dfrac{p-1}{2} \cdot \dfrac{q-1}{2}$ is even if $p \equiv 1(mod\,4)$ or $q \equiv 1(mod\,4)$, while $\dfrac{p-1}{2} \cdot \dfrac{q-1}{2}$ is odd if $p \equiv q \equiv 3(mod\,4)$. Hence,

$$\left(\frac{p}{q}\right)\left(\frac{q}{p}\right) = \begin{cases} 1, \text{ if } p \equiv 1(mod\,4) \text{ or } q \equiv 1(mod\,4) \text{ (or both)} \\ -1, \text{ if } p \equiv q \equiv 3(mod\,4) \end{cases} \tag{1.9}$$

Since the only possible values of $\left(\dfrac{p}{q}\right)$ and $\left(\dfrac{q}{p}\right)$ are ± 1. Therefore,

$$\left(\frac{p}{q}\right) = \begin{cases} \left(\dfrac{q}{p}\right), \text{ if } p \equiv 1(mod\,4) \text{ or } q \equiv 1(mod\,4) \text{ (or both)} \\ -\left(\dfrac{q}{p}\right), \text{ if } p \equiv q \equiv 3(mod\,4) \end{cases} \tag{1.10}$$

1.1.7.2 Jacobi symbol

The Jacobi symbol is the generalization of the Legendre symbol and is formally defined as follows:

Let n be a positive integer with prime factorization $n = p_1^{t_1} p_2^{t_2} \ldots p_m^{t_m}$ and let a be a positive integer relatively prime to n. Then the Jacobi symbol $\left(\dfrac{a}{n}\right)$ is defined by:

$$\left(\frac{a}{n}\right) = \left(\frac{a}{p_1^{t_1} p_2^{t_2} \ldots p_m^{t_m}}\right) = \left(\frac{a}{p_1}\right)^{t_1} \left(\frac{a}{p_2}\right)^{t_2} \ldots \left(\frac{a}{p_m}\right)^{t_m} \qquad (1.11)$$

For example: $\left(\dfrac{2}{45}\right) = \left(\dfrac{2}{3^2 \cdot 5}\right) = \left(\dfrac{2}{3}\right)^2 \left(\dfrac{2}{5}\right) = (-1)^2 (-1) = -1$ and $\left(\dfrac{109}{385}\right) = \left(\dfrac{109}{5 \cdot 7 \cdot 11}\right) =$

$\left(\dfrac{109}{5}\right)\left(\dfrac{109}{7}\right)\left(\dfrac{109}{11}\right) = \left(\dfrac{4}{5}\right)\left(\dfrac{4}{7}\right)\left(\dfrac{10}{11}\right) = \left(\dfrac{2}{5}\right)^2 \left(\dfrac{2}{7}\right)^2 \left(\dfrac{-1}{11}\right) = (-1)^2 (1)(-1) = -1.$

The above discussion regarding number theory concepts is an essential prerequisite for understanding the cryptographic algorithms [4], [5].

1.2 ABSTRACT ALGEBRA

Abstract algebra [6], [7] represents a class of powerful mathematical tools which have application in diverse fields. It is an extension of classical algebra which deals with abstract structures like groups, rings and fields instead of the usual number system. In this section, we will have an overview of these structures which is a prerequisite in understanding the core of cryptosystems.

An algebraic structure is characterized by the following three components:

- An underlying set, which is often called the carrier set of the algebraic structure.
- Operations defined on the elements of the underlying set.
- Distinguished elements of the set called the constants of the algebraic structure.

For example: $(\mathbb{Z}, +, 0)$ is an algebraic structure, where $\mathbb{Z} =$ Set of integers, $+ =$ Binary operation (Mapping from $\mathbb{Z}^2 \to \mathbb{Z}$), $\mathbb{Z}^2$ means the operation is applied between the two elements of the set $\mathbb{Z}$ and the resulting element also belongs to the set $\mathbb{Z}$, $0 =$ Constant of algebra.

In general, the operator may take m elements: $S^m \to S$, here, m is called the arity of the operation. Any two algebraic structures may have the same signature, same number of operations with the same arity and the same number of constants. For example, $(\mathbb{Z}, +, \cdot, -, 1, 0)$ and $(\mathbb{R}, +, \cdot, -, 1, 0)$, here $\mathbb{R}$ is the set of real numbers. The two algebras having the same signature may not have the same property. $(\mathbb{Z}, -, 0)$ and $(\mathbb{Q}, +, 0)$. Here, commutative law holds for the second but not for the first.

> *Sub-Algebraic Structure*: Let $A = \,<\, S, \circ, \vartriangle, k >$ *and* $A' = (S', \circ', \vartriangle' k')$ be two algebras then A' is a subalgebra of A if i) $S' \subseteq S$, ii) $a \circ' b = a \circ b$, $\forall a, b \in S'$, iii) $\vartriangle'a =_\vartriangle a$, $\forall a \in S'$ and iv) $k' = k$. If A' is subalgebra of A then A' has the same signature as A and obeys the same axioms.
>
> *Zero and One Element*: Let $\circ$ be a binary operation on S. An element $1 \in S$ is an identity for operation $\circ$ if for every $x \in S$, $1_l \circ x = x \circ 1_r = x$. An element $0 \in S$ is a zero for operation $\circ$ if for every $x \in S$, $0_l \circ x = x \circ 0_r = 0$.

Consider the following algebraic structure: $= \{a, b, c\}$, operation: $\circ$, group

table:
$$
\begin{array}{c|ccc}
\circ & a & b & c \\
\hline
a & a & b & b \\
b & a & b & c \\
c & a & b & c \\
\end{array}
$$
. Find zeros and ones.

> *Solution*: Right zero $= a, b$, No left zero, Left Identity $= b$, No right identity.
>
> *Theorem*: Let $\circ$ be a binary operation on S with left identity 1_l and right identity 1_r. Then $1_l = 1_r$ and this is referred as a two-sided identity.
>
> *Proof*: From left identity: $1_l \circ x = x$ Put $x = 1_r$. From right identity: $1_l \circ 1_r = 1_r$. $x \circ 1_r = x$ Put $x = 1_l$, $1_l \circ 1_r = 1_l$. Hence $1_r = 1_l$.

1.2.1 Semigroup

A semigroup is an algebraic structure with signature $< S, \circ >$. Semigroups usually consist of algebraic structures with single binary operation and satisfy the closure and associative properties. For example: $< \mathbb{Z}, + >, < \mathbb{Z}, \cdot >, < \mathbb{R}, + >$, $< \Sigma^*, concatenation >$.

1.2.2 Monoid

A monoid is an algebraic structure with signature $< S, \circ, 1 >$ where $\circ$ is a binary associative operation and 1 is a two-sided identity for operation $\circ$. It satisfies the closure, associative and identity axioms. Examples of monoids include: $< \mathbb{Z}, +, 0 >, < \mathbb{Z}, \cdot, 1 >, < \mathbb{R}, +, 0 >, < \Sigma^*, concatenation, \lambda >$.

1.2.3 Group

A group is an algebraic structure with signature $< S, \circ, 1, - >$ where $\circ$ is a binary associative operation and constant 1 is a two-sided identity for operation $\circ$ and $-$ is a unary operation defined over the carrier such that $\forall x \in S$, $\bar{x}$ is an inverse of x w.r.t. $\circ$. It satisfies the closure, associative, identity and inverse axioms. Examples of the group includes: $< \mathbb{Z}, +, 0, - >$, here, $-$ represents unary minus. If $\circ$ operation is commutative then the group is known as an abelian group. Groups are the most commonly used algebraic structure in the construction of cryptosystems. Therefore, we will try to cover as much detail as possible keeping in mind the page limit.

The groups possess a unique inverse: Let element a of the group have two inverses b and c, $b \circ a = e$ and $c \circ a = e$, which implies $b \circ a = c \circ a \Rightarrow b \circ a \circ b = c \circ a \circ b$. Let $a \circ b = d$, $b \circ d = c \circ d$. Now, we know each element in the group has an inverse, $b \circ d \circ d^{-1} = c \circ d \circ d^{-1} \Rightarrow b \circ e = c \circ e$. Therefore, $b = c$.

The left and right cancellation is permitted in groups because of the existence of inverses.

1.2.3.1 Symmetric finite group

The symmetric finite group is defined over the finite set $n \in \mathbb{N} = \{1, 2, 3, 4, \ldots\ldots, n\}$ and is often represented as S_n. For construction of symmetric groups, we have to consider the set permutation of n elements and give each permutation a name. These permutations will be the elements of group S_n and then we have to define the composition law. For example:

$S_1 = \{i\}$ Permutation for S_1:

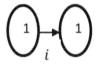

Composition law for S_1:

$\circ$	i
i	i

$S_2 = \{i, \tau\}$ Permutations for S_2:

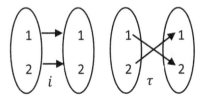

Composition law for S_2:

$\circ$	i	τ
i	i	τ
τ	τ	i

The order of S_n is the number of elements in S_n and it is the number of permutations possible with n elements which is $n!$. The symmetric groups from S_3 onwards are not abelian.

1.2.3.2 Group isomorphism

To understand the concept of group isomorphism, consider the following two groups: $G: S_2 = \{i, \tau\}$ $G' = \{+1, -1\}$

```
○ i τ × +1 −1

i i τ +1 +1 −1

τ τ i −1 −1 +1
```

The composition table of G and G' look similar and by relabeling of symbols we can turn G into G', i.e. $i \rightarrow +1$ and $\tau \rightarrow -1$. We have seen that G and G' have exact same algebraic structure, we are only using different symbols. Isomorphism is a relabeling function (φ) which preserves the group structure, $\varphi: G \rightarrow G'$ (bijective mapping – surjective and injective). It is not necessary that groups having the same order are isomorphic. Collecting all the groups that are isomorphic to one another together forms the isomorphism class. If two groups share the same isomorphism class, this means they are isomorphic to each other.

> *Example*: $G = (\mathbb{R}, +)$, where $\mathbb{R}$ is the set of real numbers and G is an abelian group. Consider another group $G' = (\mathbb{R}^+, \times)$, where $\mathbb{R}^+$ is the set of positive real numbers and G' is also an abelian group. Now, we need to define a bijective map, $\varphi: G \rightarrow G'$ from G to G' $\varphi: x \rightarrow e^x$, $\forall x \in G$ and e_G is mapped to $e_{G'}$ ($0 \rightarrow 1$). Hence G and G' are isomorphic ($G \approx G'$).

1.2.3.3 Subgroup

The subset $H \subset G$ of a group G is called subgroup $H \prec G$ of G if it is closed under composition. It is not necessary that all subsets of G form a group, so we have to cleverly choose the elements of H. The associativity axiom is trivial to prove. The identity element must be included in H from G. Each element in H should have its inverse $\forall h \in H$, $\exists h^{-1} \in H$, such that $hh^{-1} = e = h^{-1}h$.

> *Example of subgroups*: Trivial cases includes i) $G =$ Entire group G, ii) $H = \{e\}$. Other than trivial cases: $(\mathbb{Z}, +)$ is a known abelian group. Consider a set containing integer multiples of a, $a\mathbb{Z} = \{az | \forall z \in \mathbb{Z}\} = \{0, a, -a, 2a, -2a, 3a, -3a, \ldots\ldots\}$. Clearly, $a\mathbb{Z} \prec \mathbb{Z}$. If $a = 0$, $a\mathbb{Z} = \{0\}$ and if $a = 1$, $a\mathbb{Z} = \mathbb{Z}$ represents the trivial subgroups. If $a = 2$, $a\mathbb{Z} = \{0, 2, -2, 4, -4, \ldots\ldots\}$; it represents a proper subgroup which contains only even numbers. In fact, $a\mathbb{Z}$ are the only possible subgroups of $G = (\mathbb{Z}, +)$.

1.2.3.4 Intersection of subgroups

The intersection of subgroups is also a subgroup, i.e. if $H_1, H_2 \preceq G$ then $H_1 \cap H_2 \preceq G$. The intersection of two subgroups is always non-empty because it will contain at least one element, i.e. identity of group.

> *Closure*: $\forall g, \bar{g} \in H_1 \cap H_2$, we have to show: $g\bar{g} \in H_1$ and $g\bar{g} \in H_2$. We know $g, \bar{g} \in H_1$, so their composition $g\bar{g} \in H_1$. Similarly, $g\bar{g} \in H_2$. Therefore, $g\bar{g} \in H_1 \cap H_2$. Associativity: Inherited. Identity: Trivial. Inverse: $\forall g \in H_1 \cap H_2$, we need to show: $g^{-1} \in H_1 \cap H_2$. $\forall g \in H_1 \cap H_2 \rightarrow g \in H_1$ and $g \in H_2$. H_1 and H_2 are groups so $g^{-1} \in H_1$ and $g^{-1} \in H_2$.

1.2.3.5 Cyclic groups

If in a group there exists an element $x \in G$ (x is non-identity) called the generator of the group then that group is known as a cyclic group. As the name itself suggests, the generator element can generate all the elements of the group, i.e. $<x> = \{e, x^1, x^2, x^3, \ldots\ldots x^{-1}, x^{-2}, x^{-3}, \ldots\ldots\}$. The common examples of cyclic groups include, $(\mathbb{N}, +)$ and $(\mathbb{Z}, +)$.

1.2.4 Ring

So far we have seen algebraic structures with one binary operation. Ring is an algebraic structure $(A, +, \cdot)$ with two binary operations and satisfies the following conditions: i) $(A, +)$ is an abelian group, ii) $(A, \cdot)$ is a semigroup and iii) the operation $\cdot$ is distributive over the operation $+$. Example: $(Z_n, \oplus, \odot)$.

> *Division ring*: Every non-zero element has a multiplicative inverse, i.e. if $a \in R$ and $a \neq 0$ then $\exists a^{-1} \in R$: $a \cdot a^{-1} = 1 = a^{-1} \cdot a$.
>
> *Integral domain*: A commutative ring that has no zero divisors, i.e. $a \cdot b = 0 \; \forall a, b \in R$ iff $a = 0$ or $b = 0$.

1.2.5 Field

An algebraic structure $(A, +, \cdot)$ with two binary operations is called a field if the following conditions are satisfied: i) $(A, +)$ is an abelian group, ii) $(A - \{0\}, \cdot)$ is an abelian group and iii) the operation $\cdot$ is distributive over the operation $+$. Example: $(R, +, \cdot)$, $(Z_p, \oplus, \odot)$.

1.2.5.1 Finite fields

Finite fields are also known as Galois fields and have great application in the cryptography domain like the groups. Finite fields exist if the fields have p^m elements where p is prime number and m is any positive integer, i.e. the order of the finite field is either a prime or a power of prime. $GF(12)$ do not exist.

There are two types of finite fields depending upon the value of m: i) if $m = 1$, these are known as the prime fields; ii) if $m > 1$, these are known as the extension fields.

1.2.5.2 Prime fields and their arithmetic

The elements of a prime field $GF(p)$ are integers $\{0, 1, 2, ..., p-1\}$. For $a, b \in GF(p)$, we can perform addition: $(a+b) mod p$; subtraction: $(a-b) mod p$; multiplication: $(ab) mod p$; division: $(ab^{-1}) mod p$ and inversion: $a \in GF(p)$ then $aa^{-1} \equiv 1 mod p$. a^{-1} can be computed with the extended Euclidean algorithm.

1.2.5.3 Extension fields and their arithmetic

In cryptography we are mainly interested in extension fields where $p = 2$. The elements of $GF(2^m)$ are polynomials $A[X]$ of the following type:

$$a_{m-1}x^{m-1} + a_{m-2}x^{m-2} + \cdots + a_1 x + a_0 \tag{1.12}$$

where $a_i \in GF(2)$ (In general: $a_i \in GF(p) = \{0, 1, 2, ..., p-1\}$).

For example: $GF(8) = GF(2^3)$. $A[X] = a_2 x^2 + a_1 x + a_0$, where $a_i \in GF(2)$. This polynomial is considered as a vector (a_2, a_1, a_0) with possible combinations from 000 to 111.

$$GF(2^3) = \{0, 1, x, x+1, x^2, x^2+1, x^2+x, x^2+x+1\} \tag{1.13}$$

Let $A[X], B[X] \in GF(2^m)$. The addition and subtraction operation is performed as follows:

$$C[X] = A[X] + B[X] = \sum_{i=0}^{m-1} c_i x^i, \text{ where } c_i = (a_i + b_i) mod 2 \tag{1.14}$$

$$C[X] = A[X] - B[X] = \sum_{i=0}^{m-1} c_i x^i, \text{ where } c_i = (a_i - b_i) mod 2 \tag{1.15}$$

For example, $A[X] = x^2 + x + 1$ and $B[X] = x^2 + 1$. $A[X] + B[X] = (2 mod 2)x^2 + x + 2 mod 2 = x$ and $A[X] - B[X] = x$.

Note that the addition and subtraction in $GF(2^m)$ are the same operation.

For the multiplication operation it seems like multiplying two polynomials will return the correct result, i.e. $C'[X] = A[X]B[X] = (x^2 + x + 1)(x^2 + 1) = x^4 + x^3 + x + 1 \notin GF(2^m)$. However, it is not true; the resulting element does not belong to the field under consideration. Now recall prime fields: $GF(7) = \{0, 1, \ldots 6\}$, multiply the following two elements: $3.4 = 12 \bmod 7 = 5 \in GF(7)$. The correct result is obtained by computing the modulo operation. The same is the case with extension fields, we have to divide the multiplication result by a polynomial, i.e. reduce $C'[X]$ by a polynomial that behaves like a prime called an irreducible polynomial. Find the irreducible polynomial $P[X] = \sum_{i=0}^{m} p_i x^i$, where $p_i \in GF(2)$. For $GF(2^3)$: $P[X] = x^3 + x + 1$. Therefore, the correct method of multiplication in extensions fields is: $C[X] = A[X]B[X] \bmod P[X]$. For every field there exists several irreducible polynomials.

For the inversion operation in $GF(2^m)$ the extended Euclidean algorithm can be used. For example, to find the multiplication inverse of $(x^3 + x + 1) modulo (x^5 + x^3 + 1)$, use the extended Euclidean algorithm as follows:

$$x^5 + x^3 + 1 = x^2(x^3 + x + 1) + (x^2 + 1)$$

$$x^3 + x + 1 = x(x^2 + 1) + 1$$

$$x^3 + x + 1 - x(x^2 + 1) = 1$$

$$(x^3 + 1)(x^3 + x + 1) + x(x^5 + x^3 + 1) = 1$$

$$(x^3 + x + 1)^{-1} = (x^3 + 1)$$

1.2.5.4 Characteristic of a field

The characteristic of a field is a number (non-negative integer) associated with every field. It is denoted as $Ch(F)$; it is the smallest number of times the multiplicative identity (1) is added to itself to get back 0 (additive identity). For example: $F_2 = \{0, 1\}$ with the following composition table is $Ch(F) = 2(1 + 1 = 0)$.

$+$ 0 1 $*$ 0 1

0 0 1 0 0 0

1 1 0 1 0 1

Theorem: Characteristic of a field is either 0 or a prime number.

Proof: The proof is by contradiction. Let $Ch(F) = n$, where n is not a prime. Therefore, $n = ab$ such that neither of a or b is 1 and $1 < a, b < n$. By definition of characteristic of a field, $n \cdot 1 = 0$, which implies $(ab) \cdot 1 = 0$. By expanding the dot representation, $(a \cdot 1) * (b \cdot 1) = 0$. In fields there is no zero divisor, so either of $(a \cdot 1)$ or $(b \cdot 1)$ is 0. Let us say, $(a \cdot 1) = 0$. This contradicts the assumption that n is the smallest positive integer. Hence, $Ch(F) = 0 \text{ or } p$.

1.3 APPLICATION TO CRYPTOGRAPHY

These number theory and abstract algebraic [1] concepts have direct application in modern cryptography. The cryptosystems are designed in a way that involves one-way processes which are easy to compute but hard to reverse. These one-way processes are developed using the concepts in number theory. Consider the example of factoring, a very basic concept in number theory, which is a very famous example of such a one-way process in the sense that it is quite easy to multiply any two large prime, but extremely difficult to recover these prime factors given the number. This factoring problem linked with Euler's theorem forms the foundation of the most popular RSA cryptosystems. Another example of such a one-way process is the discrete logarithm problem which states that given two co-prime integers a and n and another integer k it is easy to find $a^k \bmod n$, but extremely difficult to find k, given $a^k \bmod n$. Discrete logarithm problems form the foundation of many cryptosystems and the Diffie–Hellman key exchange algorithm is the first successful example of this problem. More recently, these ideas have been extended and enriched by replacing modular arithmetic by the more exotic operations on points on elliptic curves.

1.4 CHAPTER SUMMARY

In this chapter we have discussed the fundamentals of number theory and abstract algebra which play an important role in understanding and the development of cryptosystems. Modern cryptography is totally based on the abstract algebra and number theory. Therefore, we have tried to briefly cover every aspect of these two prerequisites with respect to their application in cryptography. Further, keeping in mind the page limit as well as the clarity of concepts, we have selectively chosen topics and elaborated only those whose application can be directly seen in the cryptographic world.

REFERENCES

1. V. Shoup, *A Computational Introduction to Number Theory and Algebra*. Cambridge University Press, 2009.
2. J. J. Tattersall, *Elementary Number Theory in Nine Chapters*. Cambridge University Press, 2005.
3. A. Weil, *Basic Number Theory*, vol. 144. Springer Science & Business Media, 2013.
4. B. Gupta, D. P. Agrawal, and S. Yamaguchi, eds. *Handbook of Research on Modern Cryptographic Solutions for Computer and Cyber Security*. IGI Global, 2016.

5. P. Premkamal, S. Kumar, P. J. A. Kumar Pasupuleti, and Alphonse, "Efficient escrow-free CP-ABE with constant size ciphertext and secret key for big data storage in cloud.", *International Journal of Cloud Applications and Computing (IJCAC)*, vol. 10, no. 1, pp. 28–45, 2020.
6. C. C. Sims, *"Abstract algebra: a computational approach,"* No. 512.02 S5. J. Wiley, 1984.
7. D. S. Dummit, and R. M. Foote, *Abstract Algebra*, vol. 3. Wiley Hoboken, 2004.

Chapter 2

Introduction to cryptography

CRYPTOGRAPHY is not just an area of study but is a mandatory requirement in today's digital world. It is an essential tool for keeping digital information safe both in the system and during its transmission. If we look carefully, cryptography can be seen everywhere, from secure communication over the Internet to user authentication and to encrypting files on our disks. Cryptography resides at the heart of every system or network that needs security and privacy. Cryptography existed for thousands of years and will continue to be the basis for developing security mechanisms. This chapter covers the basic concepts related to cryptography. It briefly discusses both traditional and modern cryptography as well as the journey from conventional to modern cryptography. It describes cryptographic principles and key terms in detail to build a strong foundation.

2.1 INTRODUCTION TO CRYPTOGRAPHY

Cryptography [1]–[5] is the science of writing secrets to hide information from unintended recipients. Cryptography can do much more than establish a secret key for secure communication between different parties. Like physical signatures in our world, cryptography offers analogous, digital signatures in the digital world. The purpose of the digital signature is the same as the physical signature: it will authenticate your identity. But, unlike a physical signature, we cannot use the same digital signature to sign all the documents as we do in the physical world because in the digital world, anyone can quite easily cut and paste the digital signature to some material that we might not want to sign. Therefore, cryptography helps us to develop a digital signature which authenticates our identity while at the same time it ensures that no one can copy and paste it. It does this by making the digital signature a function of the contents of the data we want to sign. Recently, the application of cryptography has been seen in the most popular blockchain technology of the century, where one can anonymously communicate over the network. Cryptography is ancient; roughly 2078 years ago, Julius Caesar first used a very simple substitution cipher in his military commands where each letter was shifted to make the message meaningless. Later, this cipher was named after him and called the Caesar cipher. Another widespread use of cryptography in history is the Enigma machine developed by the Germans at the end of World War I and heavily used in World War II to transmit messages securely. In the next section, we will briefly discuss and categorize the famous traditional ciphers.

2.2 CLASSIFICATION OF CIPHERS

Cipher is the outcome of the conversion process from something meaningful to something scrambled and hard to understand. We expect from the reader that basic terminologies like ciphertext, plaintext, encryption, decryption, etc. are already known, and we will move directly to the different categories of ciphers and discuss them categorically as shown in Figure 2.1.

2.2.1 Based on the type of operations

The ciphers under this category care called the classical ciphers and play an important role in understanding modern ciphers.

2.2.1.1 Substitution cipher

In a substitution cipher each character in plaintext is substituted with a ciphertext character. The substitution can either be monoalphabetic, where each plaintext character is substituted with same ciphertext character, or polyalphabetic, where each plaintext character is substituted with different ciphertext characters. Examples of substitution ciphers which we will discuss include the Caesar cipher, Vigenère cipher and one-time pad.

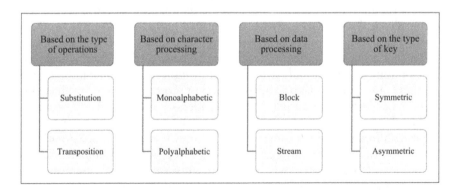

Figure 2.1 Classification of ciphers.

- Caesar cipher: This is an example of a shift cipher with the shift value fixed to three. A more flexible version of the Caesar cipher permits the shift value to be any integer. Even though an arbitrary value is allowed for the shift, there are only 25 different shift ciphers possible for any given plaintext. Since each plaintext character is always substituted with the same ciphertext character, this is an example of a monoalphabetic cipher.
- Vigenère cipher: This cipher is based on multiple interwoven shift ciphers based on the length of a keyword. The keyword is repeated until it becomes equal to the length of the plaintext. It is a type of polyalphabetic cipher.
- One-time pad (OTP): This cipher was designed by Vernam in 1917. It is an extension of Vigenère cipher with the following rules: i) the length of the keyword (key) is the same as the length of the plaintext, ii) the keyword is a randomly generated string of alphabets, iii) the keyword is used only once. OTP is known to have perfect secrecy, i.e., by looking at the ciphertext, absolutely nothing is revealed about the plaintext. Further, it is impossible to break using the brute force method. We can get the idea of the complexity of breaking OTP by this simple example: consider a message with five characters encrypted using OTP. To break the ciphertext by brute force, we need to try all possibilities of keys and conduct computation for 26^5, i.e., 11 881 376 combinations, and this is just for a message with five characters. Thus, for a longer message, the calculation grows exponentially with every new alphabet. However, OTP is hard to use in practice because of the long keys.

2.2.1.2 Transposition cipher

In the transposition cipher, instead of substituting different characters in plaintext, we change the location of elements to generate the ciphertext. Various types of transposition ciphers include the rail fence cipher, the row transposition cipher and the columnar transposition cipher.

2.2.2 Based on data processing

Depending upon the chunk of data the encryption algorithm takes to convert the plaintext to ciphertext, the ciphers fall under two categories: the block cipher and the stream cipher. The block cipher is generated by taking a fixed size of bits of data while the stream cipher is generated by taking a single bit of data at a time. These ciphers belong to the family of symmetric-key encryption.

2.2.2.1 Stream cipher

As we mentioned, stream ciphers take one bit at a time to covert the plaintext to the ciphertext. It is just like the one-time pad and is an attempt to make the OTP practical. In stream ciphers, instead of using a total random key, we use a pseudorandom key. The pseudorandom key is generated by the pseudorandom generator (PRG). PRG is a function that takes a small seed that may be 128 bits long (say) and expands it to a very long output string, which may be gigabytes long. Now, the question is, can stream ciphers also have perfect secrecy like the OTP? For perfect secrecy, the key length should be equal to the message length, but in the stream cipher, the actual key length is shorter than the message. Therefore, it cannot have perfect secrecy. Now, the question is, if the stream ciphers do not have perfect secrecy, then what makes them secure? The security of stream ciphers depends upon the specific PRG. The PRG must possess a property called unpredictability then the stream cipher is claimed to be secure. Unpredictability can be defined as, given the first i bits, there exists no efficient algorithm that can predict the $i+1$ bits with non-negligible advantage. The most common examples of stream ciphers include RC4 and CSS, which are old stream ciphers, and eStream and Salsa20, which are modern stream ciphers.

2.2.2.2 Block cipher

The fixed size of bits of data taken by the encryption algorithm is called a block. The commonly used block sizes in popular encryption algorithms are 64 bits, 128 bits and 256 bits. Now, what happens if the plaintext that we are encrypting is less than the block size taken by the algorithm? In this case, padding schemes are used to make the size of the plaintext equal to the block size. Block ciphers are built using the iterations. The most common examples of block ciphers include DES, 3DES and AES. The working details of these algorithms can be found in any standard book; here, we would like to mention the key highlights of these algorithms.

DES (data encryption standard): DES was designed by Horst Feistel in early 1970 at IBM and named Lucifer. In 1976, the National Bureau of Standards (NBS) adopted a variant of Lucifer submitted by IBM as a federal standard and called it a DES with a key length of 56 bits and a block length of 64 bits. In 1997, DES was broken by an exhaustive search where all the 2^{56} combinations of keys were tried to find the challenge key. After DES was broken, the first thing that came to the mind of experts was to strengthen DES against an exhaustive key search attack by artificially expanding the key size. As a result, triple-DES (3DES) was invented. The idea was to iterate DES a couple of times. 3DES uses three independent keys, each of length 56 bits, which makes the key size equals to 168 bits (56×3), but it is three times slower than DES. Now, the question is, why not double DES? If 2DES is used, then there exists an attack called meet in the middle which can try 2^{112} in a minimal time approximately equal to the exhaustive search attack on DES. DES was a widely used and popular cipher in banking and commerce until the year 2000 when AES completely replaced DES.

AES (advanced encryption standard): AES is a substitution-permutation network (SPN) and unlike the Fiestel network where half of the bits remain unchanged from round to round, in SPN all the bits are changed in every single round. AES comes with three key options, 128 bits, 192 bits, and 256 bits, and the block size is fixed to 128 bits. The larger the key size the more secure is the resulting cipher; however, the number of rounds will increase with the increase in key size thus making the cipher slower. But it is still six times faster than the 3DES standard and hence completely replaced the DES and is a widely used standard nowadays.

2.2.3 Based on the type of key

On the basis of the type of the keys used for encryption and decryption, ciphers are categorized into symmetric and asymmetric ciphers. In the symmetric ciphers the same key is used for both encryption and decryption while in the asymmetric ciphers different keys are used for encryption and decryption. Examples of symmetric ciphers are block and stream ciphers and all the classical ciphers; in the asymmetric category the most famous and foremost is the cipher developed by Rivest, Shamir and Adleman (RSA algorithm). We will discuss the famous asymmetric ciphers in the section where we discuss public-key encryption techniques.

2.3 TYPES OF CRYPTOGRAPHIC TECHNIQUES

In this section, we will discuss the symmetric and asymmetric or public-key cryptographic techniques. However, the main focus will be on public-key cryptographic techniques, as we later discuss the searchable encryption schemes based on public-key cryptographic primitives.

In a typical cryptosystem, there are three main components: the key-generation algorithm, the encryption algorithm and the decryption algorithm. The role of the key-generation algorithm mainly comes in public-key cryptosystems. In symmetric-key cryptosystems the sender and the receiver of the message must agree upon the common secret key used for both encryption and decryption. For this purpose, some key-exchange algorithm must exist and one such algorithm which gained a lot of popularity is the Diffie–Hellman key-exchange algorithm [6]. To understand this algorithm, let us assume the famous Alice and Bob scenario where Alice wants to securely communicate with Bob. The key-exchange process between them is shown in Figure 2.2. Alice and Bob select the public parameters (p, α) which are known to everyone.

The public parameters which Alice and Bob decided are the order, p, of the cyclic group, Z_p, and the generator, α, of the group. In the second step shown in Figure 2.2, Alice and Bob are randomly choosing one element from the cyclic group and keep them as their secrets.

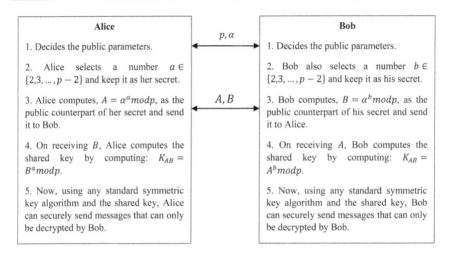

Figure 2.2 Diffie–Hellman key-exchange algorithm.

The Diffie–Hellman key-exchange algorithm suffers from man in the middle attack, where a third person intercepts all the secret messages by computing a shared secret key of its own and sending that shared secret key to both Alice and Bob. The details of this attack are left for the reader as it is readily available in any standard cryptography book. The purpose of describing the Diffie–Hellman key-exchange algorithm is to demonstrate its significance in the development of public-key cryptosystems.

The symmetric-key cryptographic techniques are much faster than public-key cryptographic techniques. On the other hand, symmetric-key techniques require the process of sharing the secret key, and this process becomes quite complicated when a large number of users want to communicate together. Take the example of cloud storage where a large number of users participate and want to share their data among themselves; in this scenario, public-key cryptography is the better choice. The searchable encryption schemes that we will discuss in the subsequent chapters are developed for cloud storage and multi-user environments. Therefore, to better understand, we need to build a strong base in the public-key cryptographic techniques.

2.3.1 Public-key cryptography

Public-key cryptography [4], also called asymmetric cryptography, contains a group of algorithms that use two different but related keys, one is used for encryption (which is called the public key) and the other is used for decryption (which is called the private key). Public-key cryptography contains the public-key encryption and signature scheme, but we will mainly focus only on the encryption schemes. In the encryption scheme, anyone who wants to communicate with someone can encrypt the message using the public key of the recipient and the recipient will use his/her corresponding private key to decrypt that message. Since the private key is only possessed by the recipient, no one else can decrypt that message. In the signature scheme, this process is inverted, to generate the signature the private key is used and to verify the signature the corresponding public key is used. The signature scheme is used to prove the authenticity and integrity of the message [7, 8, 9, and 10]. The private key is used to generate the signature of the message, which guarantees that indeed the sender has sent the message. No one can change the contents because they do not possess the private key of the original sender and therefore cannot re-encrypt the modified content of the message without revealing it to the recipient.

The public-key encryption algorithm is composed of three algorithms: the key-generation algorithm, KG, the encryption algorithm, E, and the decryption algorithm, D. The key-generation algorithm takes the security parameter, λ, and generates the public and private key pair, (pk, sk). The encryption algorithm takes the message, $m \in \mathcal{M}$ (message space) and encrypts it using the public key, pk, to generate the ciphertext, C. The decryption algorithm takes the ciphertext and the private/secret key, sk, corresponding to the public key and outputs the message, m. The decryption algorithm is obviously deterministic while the key-generation and the encryption algorithms are non-deterministic. The correctness of these algorithms can be defined as: $\forall m \in \mathcal{M} \,\& \, \forall (pk, sk) \xleftarrow{\$} KG(\lambda), D(sk, E(pk, m)) \to m.$

2.3.1.1 Security models

To prove the security of the cryptosystems, we need a formal security model which must specify the interaction mechanism followed by an adversary/attacker to interact with the legitimate users of that cryptosystem. Further, it must specify what the adversary should achieve to break the cryptosystem [11]. For example: In an encryption system the adversary may want to find the ciphertext of the messages of her choice by using something called the encryption oracle; this represents the interaction made by the adversary with the cryptosystem. Secondly, in order to break the cryptosystem, the adversary must correctly identify that the challenge ciphertext (for which the adversary has never queried before) is the encryption of the plaintext message earlier chosen by the adversary.

2.3.1.2 Security goals of a public-key cryptosystem

For any public-key encryption scheme, the following security goals must be kept in mind while designing a cryptosystem:

- Indistinguishability of encryptions/ciphertexts: This is also known as semantic security and it states that given the encryption of two messages or two ciphertexts, the adversary should not be able to distinguish between them. Simply, we can say that given a challenge ciphertext, the adversary should not be able to get any information about the underlying plaintext.

- Non-malleability: It requires that given the challenge ciphertext, the adversary should not be able to convert it into another valid ciphertext such that the plaintexts of these two ciphertexts are meaningfully related to each other.

2.3.1.3 Security attacks on a public-key cryptosystem

Depending upon the level of facilities provided to an adversary, the attacks on public-key cryptosystems are divided into three main categories:

- Chosen-plaintext attack (CPA): The facility given here is that the adversary knows the public key. The public key can be used to just encrypt the messages of her choice and the cryptography community says that the adversary has access to the encryption oracle. Later, the adversary chooses two messages of her choice, called challenge messages, which she sends to the challenger. The challenger then returns the challenge ciphertext to the adversary. Now, we say that a public-key cryptosystem is secure under CPA if it is hard for the adversary to relate the challenge ciphertext with its underlying plaintext. The restriction on the adversary is that she cannot generate the ciphertexts (have access to the encryption oracle) for the challenge messages of her choice. Here, we have restricted the power of adversary to the maximum extent. But in practice, the adversary can have much more power and thus CPA secure schemes may not be secure in practical scenarios.
- Non-adaptive chosen-ciphertext attack (CCA1): Here, the power of the adversary is increased by providing her access to the decryption oracle in addition to the facilities provided in CPA security. She can use it to get the decryption of ciphertexts of her choice. However, a restriction has been placed on when she can use the decryption oracle. Here, the adversary can use the decryption oracle only before the challenge ciphertext is produced.
- Adaptive chosen-ciphertext attack (CCA2): The restrictions of CCA1 security are completely relaxed and now the adversary can have access to the decryption oracle even after she gets the challenge ciphertext. But the obvious restriction remains that she cannot query the decryption oracle for the challenge ciphertext.

The public-key encryption schemes which are indistinguishable under CCA2 are assumed to be most secure. The reason is obvious because here the adversary can operate with full power and yet she cannot distinguish that the challenge ciphertext is the encryption of which two challenge messages generated by her.

Mathematically, this whole definition of IND-CCA2 (indistinguishability against CCA2) can be modeled as a game between the challenger, $\mathcal{C}$, and an adversary, $\mathcal{A}$ as follows:

- Setup: $\mathcal{C}$ runs $KG(\lambda) \rightarrow (pk, sk)$, keeps sk and gives pk to $\mathcal{A}$.
- Phase 1: $\mathcal{A}^D(pk, C) \rightarrow m$ and outputs two messages $\{m_0, m_1, state\}$ of her choice but she had not queried decryption oracle for them. $\mathcal{A}^D$ denotes adversary's access to decryption oracle.
- Challenge: $\mathcal{C}$ selects $\{0, 1\} \rightarrow b$, and runs encryption algorithm to get challenge ciphertext, $E(pk, m_b) \rightarrow C^*$.
- Phase 2: $\mathcal{A}^D(pk, C) \rightarrow m$ but $C \neq C^*$.
- Guess: $\mathcal{A}(C^*, m_0, m_1, state) \rightarrow b'$.

Adversary wins the game if $b' = b$, i.e. when its guess is correct. Since there are two messages, therefore with a probability of $\frac{1}{2}$, anyone can guess. Hence, we need to subtract this probability from the total probability of correctly guessing b and this is known as the adversary's advantage, $Adv_{\mathcal{A}}^{IND-CCA2}$ against IND-CCA2.

$$Adv_{\mathcal{A}}^{IND-CCA2}(\lambda) = \left| Pr[b' = b] - \frac{1}{2} \right| \tag{2.1}$$

The cryptosystem is said to be secure against CCA2 attack if the advantage of the adversary in winning the game is negligible.

2.3.1.4 ElGamal cryptosystem

The ElGamal encryption was invented in 1985 by Taher ElGamal [12] and it is very similar to the Diffie–Hellman key-exchange algorithm with a slight reordering of steps as shown in Figure 2.3.

Alice		Bob
2. Upon receiving the public parameters, p, α, β. Alice selects a number $i \in \{2, 3, \dots, p - 2\}$ and keep it as her secret and compute $K_E = \alpha^i mod p$, and $K_M = \beta^i mod p$	p, α, β	1. Choose a prime, p of size k given the security parameter, 1^k. Select an element α like in the DH key exchange algorithm. Choose $d \in \{2, 3, \dots, p - 2\}$ and compute $\beta = \alpha^d mod p$. d is kept by Bob as his secret/private key.
3. Alice uses K_M to encrypt the message X as, $Y = X \cdot K_M mod p$.		
5. Send the encrypted message with K_E to Bob.	Y, K_E	2. Bob also selects a number $b \in \{2, 3, \dots, p - 2\}$ and keep it as his secret.
		6. Bob computes, $K_M = K_E{}^d mod p$, and decrypts the message as, $X = Y \cdot$

Figure 2.3 ElGamal cryptosystem.

Here, the key K_E is called the ephemeral key and exists only for a short duration, i.e. when Alice wants to send some new message then at that time a different i value is selected which will result in a different ephemeral key. The key K_M is called the session key, which is just like the key K_{AB} in the DH key-exchange algorithm. The ElGamal encryption scheme is a probabilistic encryption scheme unlike the schoolbook RSA encryption scheme and this feature comes into the picture by choosing a random i value every time the encryption algorithm is called, whereas in RSA the encryption of the same message is always fixed.

Correctness Proof: Bob computes, $Y \cdot K_M^{-1} mod p = X \cdot K_M \cdot (K_E^{\,d})^{-1} mod p = X \cdot \beta^i \cdot (\alpha^i)^{-d} mod p = X mod p$.

We will present the detailed security analysis of this scheme in Chapter 4 where we will discuss provable security in detail.

2.4 GENERALIZATIONS IN PUBLIC-KEY CRYPTOGRAPHY

If we recall public-key encryption technique type, there are three main algorithms: key-generation, encryption and decryption. The key-generation algorithm takes the security parameter and generates a public and private key pair. The public key generated by this algorithm is completely random. In 1984 Shamir proposed an idea that instead of using the public key as a complicated random string, use something like an email address, phone number, IP address etc. which is unique for the users. This generalization of the public-key encryption is called the identity-based encryption (IBE) [13, 14, 15, 16]. So now, when Bob encrypts a message for Alice, he will use Alice's email address as the public key and Alice can use the private key generator to extract the private key corresponding to her ID, i.e. the email address in this case. Like IBE there are other generalizations to the standard public-key encryption (PKE) techniques like attribute-based encryption (ABE) [17, 18, 19, 20, 21, 22], broadcast encryption (BE) [23, 24], homomorphic encryption (HE) [25] and functional encryption (FE) [26, 27, 28, 29] as shown in Figure 2.4. Among them we will discuss IBE and ABE as we have seen a lot of application of these two techniques in the construction of searchable encryption schemes.

2.4.1 Identity-based encryption (IBE)

In IBE there are four algorithms, one additional algorithm is called the setup algorithm, S, and the other three are the same as the standard PKE.

$(PP, MSK) \leftarrow S(\lambda)$: The setup algorithm takes the security parameter and produces the public parameters, PP, and master secret key, MSK. This algorithm is generally executed by a trusted third party often called the key-generation center (KGC).

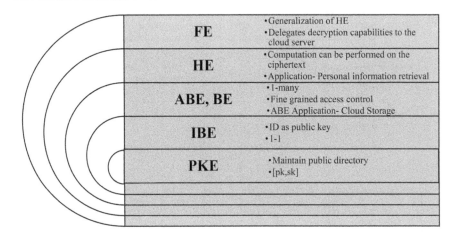

FE	• Generalization of HE • Delegates decryption capabilities to the cloud server
HE	• Computation can be performed on the ciphertext • Application- Personal information retrieval
ABE, BE	• 1-many • Fine grained access control • ABE Application- Cloud Storage
IBE	• ID as public key • 1-1
PKE	• Maintain public directory • [pk,sk]

Figure 2.4 Generalization of PKE.

$SK_{ID} \leftarrow K(MSK, ID)$: The key generator algorithm takes the MSK and ID of the user and generates his private key corresponding to his ID, i.e. SK_{ID}.

$C \leftarrow E(PP, ID, m)$: The encryption algorithm encrypts the message, m, using the public-key ID and PP and outputs the ciphertext, C.

$m \leftarrow D(SK_{ID}, C)$: The decryption algorithm decrypts the ciphertext using SK_{ID}.

Correctness Proof: The IBE scheme is said to be correct if $\forall PP$ and SK_{id} generated from *IBE_Setup*(λ), the following condition holds:

$$D(SK_{ID}, E(PP, ID, m)) = m \tag{2.2}$$

The pictorial representation of the IBE scheme can be seen in Figure 2.5.

With an IBE scheme using the single master key and the different IDs we can generate the different secret keys. Basically, in IBE an attempt has been made to compress the exponential number of public keys into one short public parameters string. The first practical IBE scheme was designed by Boneh and Franklin [30] in 2001.

2.4.2 Attribute-based encryption (ABE)

IBE is a very natural extension of PKE, like PKE using IBE, we can send the message to a single intended user. ABE is developed for a different scenario; say we have a lot of data, like an encrypted database, and we have a diverse set of users who need access to different pieces of that data and it is not necessarily their identity which determines who would access what. Instead the attributes of the users will determine their access capability. For example:

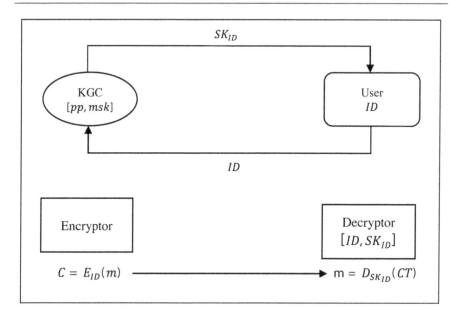

Figure 2.5 A typical IBE scheme.

we may want to provide access to the authorized users based on their type of job etc. We see this type of scenario everywhere around us. Attribute-based encryption is devised to handle such scenarios. It is one of the most popular PKE techniques. It provides fine-grained access control capabilities. Before ABE every PKE scheme was one-to-one, i.e. the encrypted message is intended for just one user. In ABE we can send the same encrypted message intended for multiple users and thus it supports the one-to-many scenario. Based on attributes either associated with the users or the data, we have two variants called key-policy attribute-based encryption (KP-ABE) and ciphertext-policy attribute-based encryption (CP-ABE). In KP-ABE, the access policy is associated with the secret key of the user and attributes are associated with the ciphertext. In CP-ABE, the access policy is associated with the ciphertext and the attributes are associated with secret key of the user. For the purpose of common presentation, let I_K denotes the input to the key-generation algorithm, K and I_E denotes the input to the encryption algorithm, E. In KP-ABE, I_K and I_E are the access policy and the set of attributes respectively. In CP-ABE, I_K and I_E are the set of attributes and the access policy respectively. Like IBE, ABE schemes also consist of four polynomial time algorithms:

$(PP, MSK) \leftarrow S(\lambda, Att)$: The setup algorithm takes the attribute universe, $Att = \{att_1, att_2, \cdots, att_{|Att|}\}$ in addition to the security parameter, λ like in IBE scheme and outputs the public parameters PP and master secret key MSK.

$SK_u \leftarrow K(PP, MSK, I_K)$: The key generator algorithm takes the MSK and the credentials of a user, I_K, and generates his private key corresponding to his credentials, i.e. SK_u.

$C \leftarrow E(PP, m \in \mathcal{M}, I_E)$: The encryption algorithm encrypts the message, m, using I_E and PP and outputs the ciphertext, C.

$m \leftarrow D(C, SK_u)$: The decryption algorithm decrypts the ciphertext using SK_u if and only if the satisfiability condition holds between I_K and I_E.

Correctness Proof: if the satisfiability condition holds between I_K and I_E, then for the given PP and MSK, the following condition must hold:

$$D(E(m, PP, I_E), SK_u) = m \tag{2.3}$$

The pictorial representation of KP-ABE scheme can be seen in Figure 2.6. Here, the user possesses a set of attributes and gets the corresponding secret key from KGC. Consider an example of an educational institute, where the department of computer engineering has released the marks of Ph.D. and M.Tech. students. The marks are uploaded on their shared storage and the department wants the marks to only be accessed by the specified candidates. Hence, they encrypt them with an access policy, $W = CE \wedge (PhD \vee MTech)$ and upload them to their shared storage. When some student with credentials, L, wants to check his/her marks, he/she will be able to decrypt if and only if L satisfies W. As we can see in the Figure 2.6, only user U_3's credentials satisfy W and hence he/she will be able to see the marks.

The ABE scheme has a security threat of collusion. For example: A job posting has been encrypted under a policy such that only the users who have both a master's degree and at least two-years of experience can decrypt. There may exists two users who individually possess only one of these attributes. So, the user with master degree but no experience should not be able to decrypt.

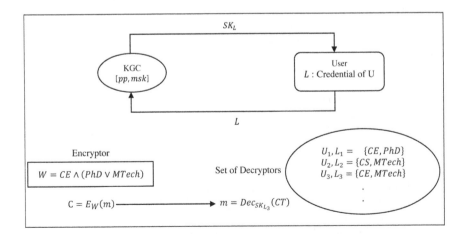

Figure 2.6 A typical CP-ABE scheme.

Similarly, the user who has the experience but no degree should also not be able to decrypt. We want to prevent the scenario where somehow these users combine their keys and try to impersonate a user who has all the required attributes. Hence, the ABE scheme should be developed in a manner that prevents users from combining their keys and learning something that neither of them individually should be able to learn, otherwise the whole purpose of ABE is defeated.

2.5 CHAPTER SUMMARY

In this chapter, we have covered the cryptographic primitives from the beginning of their history to the latest techniques which are used today. We have described how the standard PKE technique is generalized and relaxed to get other public-key cryptographic techniques. We have mainly discussed aspects related to public-key cryptography because in later chapters our focus is on construction of searchable encryption schemes based on public-key cryptographic primitives. Among the PKE techniques, identity-based encryption and attribute-based encryption are discussed in detail because of their application in searchable encryption.

REFERENCES

1. A. J. Menezes, J. Katz, P. C. Van Oorschot, and S. A. Vanstone, *Handbook of Applied Cryptography*. CRC Press, 1996.
2. W. Stallings, *Cryptography and Network Security, 4/E*. Pearson Education India, 2006.
3. K. H. Rosen, "An introduction to cryptography," *ISBN-10*, pp. 1–58488, 2007.
4. C. Paar, and J. Pelzl, *Understanding Cryptography: a Textbook for Students and Practitioners*. Springer Science & Business Media, 2009.
5. O. Goldreich, *Foundations of Cryptography: Volume 2, Basic Applications*. Cambridge University Press, 2009.
6. W. Diffie, and M. Hellman, "New directions in cryptography,", *IEEE Trans. Inf. Theory*, vol. 22, no. 6, pp. 644–654, 1976.
7. B. B. Gupta, and M. Quamara, "An identity based access control and mutual authentication framework for distributed cloud computing services in IoT environment using smart cards", *Procedia Comput. Sci*, vol. 132, pp. 189–197, 2018.
8. A. Tewari, and B. B. Gupta, "A novel ECC-based lightweight authentication protocol for internet of things devices", *Int. J. High Perform. Comput. Networking*, vol. 15, no. 1–2, pp. 106–120, 2019.
9. Q. Zheng, X. Wang, M. K. Khan, W. Zhang, B. B. Gupta, and W. Guo, "A lightweight authenticated encryption scheme based on chaotic scml for railway cloud service", *IEEE Access*, vol. 6, pp. 711–722, 2017.
10. B. B. Gupta, and T. Aakanksha. *A Beginner's Guide to Internet of Things Security: Attacks, Applications, Authentication, and Fundamentals*. CRC Press, 2020.

11. B. B. Gupta, G. M. Perez, D. P. Agrawal, and D. Gupta. *Handbook of Computer Networks and Cyber Security*. Springer Science and Business Media LLC, 2020.

12. T. ElGamal, "A public key cryptosystem and a signature scheme based on discrete logarithms," *IEEE Trans. Inf. Theory*, vol. 31, no. 4, pp. 469–472, 1985.

13. D. Khader, "Public Key Encryption with Keyword Search Based on K-Resilient IBE," in *International Conference on Computational Science and Its Applications*, 2007, pp. 1086–1095.

14. D. Boneh, and X. Boyen, "Secure Identity Based Encryption without Random Oracles," in *Annual International Cryptology Conference*, 2004, pp. 443–459.

15. D. Boneh, X. Boyen, and E.-J. Goh, "Hierarchical Identity Based Encryption With Constant Size Ciphertext," in *Annual International Conference on the Theory and Applications of Cryptographic Techniques*, 2005, pp. 440–456.

16. S. Kaushik, and C. Gandhi, "Ensure hierarchal identity based data security in Cloud environment," *Int. J. Cloud Appl. Comput*, vol. 9, no. 4, pp. 21–36, 2019.

17. J. Bethencourt, A. Sahai, and B. Waters, "Ciphertext-Policy Attribute-Based Encryption," in *2007 IEEE symposium on security and privacy (SP'07)*, 2007, pp. 321–334.

18. V. Goyal, A. Jain, O. Pandey, and A. Sahai, "Bounded ciphertext policy attribute based encryption," in *International Colloquium on Automata, Languages, and Programming*, 2008, pp. 579–591.

19. V. Goyal, O. Pandey, A. Sahai, and B. Waters, "Attribute-Based Encryption for Fine-Grained Access Control of Encrypted Data," in *Proceedings of the 13th ACM conference on Computer and communications security*, 2006, pp. 89–98.

20. Y. Jiang, W. Susilo, Y. Mu, and F. Guo, "Ciphertext-policy attribute-based encryption against key-delegation abuse in fog computing," *Futur. Gener. Comput. Syst*, vol. 78, pp. 720–729, 2018.

21. M. Chase, and S. S. M. Chow, "Improving Privacy and Security in Multi-Authority Attribute-Based Encryption," in *Proceedings of the 16th ACM conference on Computer and communications security*, 2009, pp. 121–130.

22. P. K. Premkamal, S. K. Pasupuleti, and P. J. A. Alphonse, "Efficient escrow-free CP-ABE with constant size ciphertext and secret key for big data storage in cloud," *Int. J. Cloud Appl. Comput*, vol. 10, no. 1, pp. 28–45, 2020.

23. Z. Zhou, and D. Huang, "On Efficient Ciphertext-Policy Attribute Based Encryption and Broadcast Encryption," in *Proceedings of the 17th ACM conference on Computer and communications security*, 2010, pp. 753–755.

24. C. Delerablée, "Identity-Based Broadcast Encryption With Constant Size Ciphertexts and Private Keys," in *International Conference on the Theory and Application of Cryptology and Information Security*, 2007, pp. 200–215.

25. C. Gentry, "Fully homomorphic encryption using ideal lattices," in *In Proc. STOC*, 2009, pp. 169–178.

26. S. Agrawal, X. Boyen, V. Vaikuntanathan, P. Voulgaris, and H. Wee, "Functional encryption for threshold functions (or fuzzy IBE) from lattices," in *International Workshop on Public Key Cryptography*, 2012, pp. 280–297.

27. D. Boneh, A. Raghunathan, and G. Segev, "Function-Private Identity-Based Encryption: Hiding the Function in Functional Encryption," in *Annual Cryptology Conference*, 2013, pp. 461–478.

28. D. Boneh, A. Sahai, and B. Waters, "Functional Encryption: Definitions and Challenges," in *Theory of Cryptography Conference*, 2011, pp. 253–273.

29. N. Attrapadung, and B. Libert, "Functional encryption for inner product: Achieving constant-size ciphertexts with adaptive security or support for negation," in *International Workshop on Public Key Cryptography*, 2010, pp. 384–402.

30. D. Boneh, and M. Franklin, "Identity-Based Encryption from the Weil Pairing," in *Annual international cryptology conference*, 2001, pp. 213–229.

Chapter 3

Searchable encryption and data management

SEARCHABLE ENCRYPTION (SE) is a technique that allows search operations in the encrypted domain without disclosing any information about what is being searched. Searchable encryption acts as a data management technique that allows the data owners to store and manage their data at a third-party, untrusted cloud server and allows the data user to delegate search functionality to the cloud server to retrieve that data. Hence, searchable encryption enables the secure storage and retrieval of data at the optimized cost. Searchable encryption has application in the scenario where we want both confidentiality and accessibility. In addition to its direct use in searching encrypted data, searchable encryption has also changed the way any encryption technique can work. Generally, an encryption technique either decrypts the complete data or none of it, which makes it unsuitable for situations where only a part of the data needs to be decrypted. To design such a flexible system, the searchable encryption technique can be used where one can search a particular part of the encrypted data and thereby can achieve partial decryption.

3.1 NEED FOR SEARCHABLE ENCRYPTION

In recent times, we have seen a significant shift towards cloud storage. Cloud storage is emerging as a promising alternative to local storage. More and more firms are opting for the cloud paradigm, as all of the overhead of maintenance of storage is delegated to the cloud server [1, 2]. Further, in contrast to local storage, the data stored in the cloud can be accessed anywhere and at any time as long as you have Internet access [3, 4]. Apart from such advantages of cloud storage, there are some concerns which are inherently associated with cloud storage, and privacy issues are the most prominent among them [5, 6]. The data is stored over a third-party server which cannot be trusted with security of sensitive data [7, 8]. Theoretically, data privacy concern could be easily resolved by storing the data in an encrypted form [4, 5]. However, although encryption solves the problem of privacy [9, 10, 11], it also engenders some other serious issues including infeasibility of the fundamental search operation, reduction in flexibility of sharing the data with other users etc. To address these issues, the concept of searchable encryption was introduced. Searchable encryption allows a third-party cloud server to perform search on encrypted data without disclosing any information about what is being searched. Secure searchable encryption is the answer to this need [7, 12].

3.2 GENERAL MODEL

The searchable encryption technique allows a server to search in encrypted data on behalf of a client without disclosing information about the plaintext data. There are few schemes that implement searchable encryption by making the ciphertext itself searchable [1]; most of the schemes generate an encrypted index which is searchable. The searchable encrypted index can be generated by exacting the metadata items $W = (w_1, ..., w_m)$ from the main data file and encrypting them using a technique which enables search operation over this index. This operation is performed by executing the encryption algorithm defined in the searchable encryption scheme (E_{SE}). These metadata items are often called the keywords in searchable encryption terminology. The main data file is also encrypted with any standard symmetric-key encryption, E_{Symm}, as shown in Figure 3.1. The symmetric key used for this purpose may be encrypted with the same encryption technique which we used for generating the index.

The encrypted index and the encrypted data file are then stored on a cloud server that is generally assumed to be honest but curious, i.e. it can be trusted to correctly perform storage and query protocols, however, it tries to learn as much information as possible. This whole task is done by an entity named the data owner. Now, another entity called the data user wants to retrieve the encrypted information stored at the cloud server. Obviously, he/she needs to first search among the data files to retrieve what he/she needs. The data

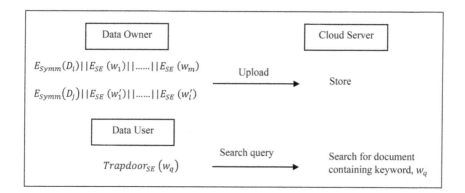

Figure 3.1 General model of a searchable encryption scheme.

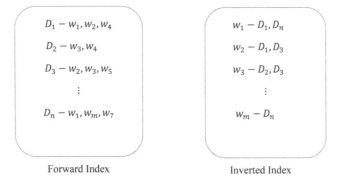

$$D_1 - w_1, w_2, w_4$$
$$D_2 - w_3, w_4$$
$$D_3 - w_2, w_3, w_5$$
$$\vdots$$
$$D_n - w_1, w_m, w_7$$

$$w_1 - D_1, D_n$$
$$w_2 - D_1, D_3$$
$$w_3 - D_2, D_3$$
$$\vdots$$
$$w_m - D_n$$

Forward Index   Inverted Index

Figure 3.2 Approaches to generate index.

user delegates this search operation to the cloud server by generating a search trapdoor or sometimes called a search token for the keyword he/she is looking for, by using the trapdoor algorithm defined in the searchable encryption scheme (*Trapdoor$_{SE}$*) and sends it to the cloud server. Using the search trapdoor, the cloud server is now able to perform search in the encrypted domain and returns the reference to the file which contains the queried keyword without actually decrypting anything.

To generate the index, generally there are two approaches, the forward approach and the inverted approach as shown in Figure 3.2. In the forward approach, an index is built over the data files $(D_1, D_2,..., D_n)$, i.e. to each data file some keywords are associated. In the inverted approach, an index is built over the keywords $(w_1, w_2,..., w_m)$, i.e. it indexes each keyword belongs to that data file.

In the forward-index approach, the search time varies linearly with the number of data file. In the inverted-index approach, the search time varies with the of number of documents containing a particular keyword and it can be reduced to sublinear if a hash tree approach is used to build the index. One of the approaches is followed while developing a searchable encryption technique but generally it is not shown explicitly in the construction. The only focus of a searchable encryption scheme is to encrypt the associated metadata (keywords) with the data file in an efficient way.

3.3 BROAD CATEGORIZATION OF SEARCHABLE ENCRYPTION SCHEMES

Searchable encryption schemes can be developed using either symmetric key or public-key encryption. In the cloud storage environment, public-key setting is a preferable choice as there are multiple users who can have access to the shared storage and symmetric-key encryption requires key distribution among these users which is a very complicated process, whereas in the public-key setting no such key sharing is required. Therefore, considering the shared cloud storage environment, this book mainly discusses the searchable encryption schemes developed using public-key cryptographic primitive. However, in this chapter, we will mention some pioneering work done in the area of searchable encryption in the symmetric key and discuss some of them in the public-key setting.

3.3.1 Symmetric searchable encryption

Symmetric-key primitives allow a single user to read and write data, and allows only the secret key holder to create searchable ciphertexts and trap-doors [13]. The immediate application of symmetric searchable encryption (SSE) can be seen in the scenario where some user wants to store his/her data on the cloud storage in an encrypted form and later he/she can perform search on it to retrieve the required data [14]. The index approach is explicitly mentioned and addressed in the SSE schemes only. The first SSE was proposed by Song et al. [15]. The proposed scheme supports equality query and was developed to handle just one keyword. To encrypt the data, first they break it into fixed size blocks called words and then each word is encrypted independently by inserting a hash value in the specific format. The ciphertext resulting from this process is itself searchable. The cloud server performs search by extracting the hash and looking for the specific format indicated by the user. However, this scheme has a restriction that it needs to break the data into fixed size words which are incompatible with the existing encryption standard. Further, they did not provide any formal security definition or security proof for their scheme. Later, in 2003 Goh [16] relaxed the fixed size restriction in the Song et al. scheme. They used a direct index approach where an index is built for every data file using bloom filters. In 2005, Chang and Mitzenmacher [17] developed a SSE scheme and, like the Goh scheme, they used a direct index approach where an index is built based on the dictionary of search keywords instead of bloom filters, which inherently have very high false positive rate. In 2006, Curtmola et al. [18] for the first time used an inverted-index approach and achieved the sublinear search time. The comparative analysis of these pioneer works in the domain of SSE in terms of computational complexity and key feature is given below in Table 3.1.

We mentioned earlier that we are considering a cloud storage environment where the data owner may want to share his/her data and is not merely storing it for his/her own use. Indeed, the symmetric-key encryption is fast, but in the scenario which we are considering, the symmetric-key encryption becomes quite complicated due to the distribution of the secret keys to all the users. Therefore, we will discuss searchable encryption in the public-key setting with great detail in Chapter 5 and an overview is presented in the subsequent section.

Table 3.1 Comparative analysis of pioneering works in the SSE domain

Scheme	Encryption time	Trapdoor time	Search time	Feature
Song et al. [15]	$D \cdot K$	k	$D \cdot K$	Sequential scan
Chang & Mitzenmacher [17]	$D(K + K'')$	$2k$	D	Dictionary of search keywords
E. J. Goh [16]	$D \cdot K'$	k	$D \cdot k$	Bloom Filter index
Curtmola et al. [18]	$3K'' \cdot D + D(w)$	$2k$	$D(w)$	Sublinear search time

Notes:

D — Number of documents
K — Number of keywords per document
K' — Number of distinct keywords per document
K'' — Number of distinct keywords in database
k — Number of keywords per trapdoor

3.3.2 Searchable encryption in public-key setting

The public-key cryptographic primitives like identity-based encryption and attribute-based encryption are developed using a tool called bilinear maps and often such schemes are called pairing-based cryptographic schemes. The searchable encryption schemes in a public-key setting will obviously use this tool. Therefore, before we start our discussion on public-key based searchable encryption schemes, let us discuss some interesting facts about this powerful tool first.

3.3.2.1 Bilinear map

Bilinear map is a function which maps elements from one cyclic group to elements in another cyclic group. Bilinear maps are often called bilinear pairings because they take a pair of two elements from the source group and map that pair to an element in the target group.

Let G_1, G_2 be the source cyclic groups of prime order, p, and G_T be the target cyclic group of same prime order, p, and g, h be the generators of the source group, G_1, and G_2 respectively. Let e be a map between G_1 and G_2, $e\colon G_1 \times G_2 \to G_T$, it is called a bilinear map if it satisfies the following conditions:

- $\forall\, X = g^u \in G_1$ and $Y = h^v \in G_2$: $e(g^u, h^v) = e(g, h)^{uv}$ where $u, v \in Z_p$. This is called the bilinearity property.
- $e(g, h)$ is the generator of the target group, G_T, if g, h are the generators of source groups G_1 and G_2 respectively. This property is called non-degeneracy.
- $\forall\, X \in G_1$ and $Y \in G_2$; $e(l, m)$ is efficiently computable.

If e maps every pair to the identity element in G_T, then we say the bilinear map is degenerate, i.e. if there is only first condition then it also allows degenerate maps. Therefore, the second is added to make the bilinear map valid.

3.3.2.1.1 Relation between the source and the target groups in e

Among all the source and the target groups there exists isomorphism, since all of them are cyclic and have the same order. However, they possess different elements and the operation between the elements may also be different which makes them distinct from each other. If $G_1 = G_2$, i.e. both the source groups are exactly identical, then the associated map is called the symmetric bilinear map and if both are different, then the associated map is called the asymmetric bilinear map. Further, the order of the source and the target groups may also be composite instead of some prime, p. Most of the constructions consider prime order groups, some examples do exist in the literature which consider composite order groups. If the source and the target groups are all equal, then the associated map is called self bilinear map. Such maps do not exist and it is an open problem to build one.

In some existing works, another notation has been seen where the bilinearity property is expressed as $e(uX, vY) =$ instead of $e(X^u, Y^v)$, where X, Y are the elements of the source groups. This case is seen when the groups are written additively, however the multiplicative notation is more popular.

3.3.2.1.2 How the source and target groups are chosen

For the source groups, typically an elliptic curve over some finite field, F_p is used. There are different types of pairing, type A, A1, D, E, F and G [19] that result from choosing elliptic curves of different embedding degree. While the target group is generally a finite field.

The Weil [20] and Tate [21, 22] pairing are the only known example of bilinear pairing. The Weil pairing was practically used by Boneh and Franklin [23] in the construction of an identity-based encryption scheme.

3.3.2.2 The first pioneering SE scheme in a public-key setting

Boneh et al. [24] developed the first searchable encryption in a public-key setting called public-key encryption with keyword search and is famous by name, PEKS. Among the available public-key cryptographic primitives, they used identity-based encryption (IBE) as an underlying scheme. They used the public key corresponding to the user's identity to encrypt the data file and the keywords contained in the data file. The scheme was developed for the efficient retrieval of encrypted emails from the email server. The data owner or more appropriately the sender wants to send an email encrypted under the public key of the recipient along with the keywords encrypted under the same key. The sent email gets stored at the email server of the recipient and the recipient needs a mechanism to efficiently retrieve only the desired emails among them. This efficient mechanism is the technique of searchable encryption, without which the recipient first needs to download all the emails and then decrypt them locally using his/her private key. But with the searchable encryption technique, the recipient can extract the emails according to his current requirement and needs to decrypt only those selected emails. This whole mechanism is suitable in those scenarios where we have a single intended recipient; however, there is no restriction upon the number of senders. Now, if we want to send the same message to multiple recipients, can we apply the same mechanism as discussed above? The answer is, yes. However, it will not be an efficient mechanism. To send the same message to multiple recipients, we need to encrypt the same message multiple times with the public key of each recipient and this leads to a lot of redundancy in the system. Since we want an efficient mechanism, there is a need to explore other cryptographic primitives like attribute-based encryption (ABE) which may possibly resolve this redundancy and we will discuss such schemes in Chapter 5 which is dedicated to searchable encryption in public-key setting.

3.3.2.2.1 PEKS insights

Consider the famous cryptographic example of Alice and Bob where Bob wants to send an email message, $m \in \mathcal{M}$, along with several keywords, $\{w_1, w_2, ..., w_l\} \in W$ to Alice. These associated keywords are later used to search the corresponding email message. Bob generates the following ciphertext: $E_{A_{pub}}(m) \| PEKS(A_{pub}, w_1) \| ... \| PEKS(A_{pub}, w_l)$ where $E_{A_{pub}}(m)$ is any standard public-key encryption algorithm which uses public key of Alice, A_{pub} to generate the encrypted email message and PEKS is an algorithm which supports keyword search. The generated ciphertext is stored at Alice's email server. To perform search, Alice uses her secret key/private key to generate a secret for a particular keyword she wants to search and that secret is known as the search trapdoor/token. The email server will use this trapdoor and finds the message which contains this keyword using the search algorithm. The search algorithm returns a binary output 1 if a matching keyword is found, otherwise it returns 0. The details of the algorithms involved in the PEKS scheme are given in Table 3.2.

As we stated, the PEKS is based on the IBE scheme. Now, let us examine how. The K_{pub} plays the role of public parameters and the K_{pri} acts just like the master secret key in a typical IBE scheme. The IBE ciphertext is generated using the public parameters, i.e. K_{pub} and the keyword, w, here acts as an identity. In the trapdoor algorithm, shown in step 3, basically a secret key is generated for the ID, which is w in the present scheme. This step is just like getting the secret key for the ID in an IBE scheme. The search algorithm is like the decryption algorithm in an IBE scheme which takes the ciphertext and the secret key, i.e. the trapdoor in the present scheme.

Table 3.2 Public-key encryption with keyword search (PEKS) [24]

PEKS Scheme

The PEKS scheme uses two hash functions, H_1, H_2, and a symmetric bilinear map, $e: G_1 \times G_1 \to G_T$, where G_1 and G_T are cyclic groups of prime order, p.

1. *Key Generation:* Randomly choose $\alpha \in Z_p^*$, and find g be the generator of G_1. Compute, $K_{pub} = (g, h = g^\alpha)$ and $K_{pri} = \alpha$.

2. *PEKS* (K_{pub}, w): Randomly choose $r \in Z_p^*$, and compute, $t = e(H_1(w), h^r)$. Output, $C = [g^r, H_2(t)]$.

3. *Trapdoor* (K_{pri}, w): Output, $T_w = H_1(w)^\alpha \in G_1$.

4. *Search* (C, T_w): Test if $H_2(e(T_w, g^r)) = H_2(t)$, if yes, a match has been found and returns 1; otherwise; returns 0.

PEKS Highlights

- No interaction between sender and the receiver.
- Supports multiple data owner (sender) and single data user (recipient) popularly known as M/S setting [25].
- It has application in secure email retrieval.
- Suitable for polynomial size keyword space.
- PEKS is secure against adaptive chosen keyword attack under the Bilinear Diffie–Hellman (BDH) assumption in random oracle model.
- Email server is assumed to be honest and curious, i.e. it correctly executes all algorithms but it may try to learn some useful information.

PEKS Limitations

- Requires secure channel to prevent eavesdropping.
- To support multiple data users, same message encrypted with the public key of each intended user is sent which leads to redundancy.
- Since the keyword space is small, the PEKS and all the public-key searchable encryption schemes suffers from keyword-guessing attack (KGA) [26] unless it is explicitly handled.
- PEKS was designed for one-time use. The server may memorize the trapdoor and use it to get information about future emails.
- Does not support multi-keyword search.

The security-related definitions stated in the above points will be explained in detail in the next chapter. The two main drawbacks of PEKS, the secure channel requirement between server and data user and the KGA remained the focus of the work after PEKS which are discussed in the subsequent sections.

3.3.2.2.2 Secure channel-free PEKS

Building a secure channel to send the trapdoor is quite expensive, therefore efforts have been made to remove this restriction and make the trapdoor secure enough to send on some public channel.

BSS2: Baek et al. [27] proposed the first secure channel-free PEKS scheme. The authors resolved the flaw in the design of the PEKS scheme where the server may use the stored trapdoors and perform search by itself without the knowledge of the recipient. The trivial solution to this problem is to restrict the use of the keywords only once. However, this solution is not practical if the user wants to reuse the keywords. Baek et al. [27] suggested a solution where the keywords are periodically refreshed and this is done by attaching time-period information; the user appends the time period for which he wants to generate the trapdoor. They named this process as refreshing keywords. For example, if data user wants to generate a trapdoor for a keyword say, URGENT, then before generating its trapdoor the user will first append it with the time period as follows: URGENT‖01/08/2019.

Further, to remove the secure channel Baek et al. [27] used a public-private key pair (PK,SK) for the server. In addition to the PEKS algorithms, SCF_PEKS possesses an extra algorithm for generating the key pair for the server. To generate the keyword ciphertext they will use the public key of the receiver as well as the public key of the server. To generate the ciphertext the SCF_PEKS scheme will use the secret key of the receiver like in the PEKS scheme. Finally, there is a slight difference in the search algorithm; in addition to the keyword ciphertext and trapdoor, it takes the secret key of the server to ensure security from an outside attacker.

They ensured security from a malicious server as well as an outside attacker. The malicious server cannot distinguish between the ciphertext of two keywords until it has the trapdoor for that keyword. Similarly, the outside attacker cannot distinguish between ciphertext of two keywords even if he has the trapdoor of all the keywords because he does not have the server's secret key.

GZP: Gu et al. [28] proposed another PEKS scheme which is free from the requirement of secure channels. Like the SCF_PEKS scheme proposed by Baek et al. [27], this scheme uses both the receiver's public key as well as the server's public key to generate the keyword ciphertext, the receiver's secret key to generate the trapdoor and in the search algorithm it also uses the secret key of the cloud server. The authors have developed two searchable encryption schemes. In the first scheme, no pairing operation is used to generate the keyword ciphertext and the trapdoor. In the second scheme, no pairing operation is used to generate the trapdoor and also removes secure channel restriction, which makes it computationally efficient.

FSG⁺: Another secure channel-free PEKS scheme was proposed by Fang et al. [29]. Like SCF_PEKS and SCF_PEKS2, this scheme also generates separate public and private keys for the server. Their scheme is based Gentry's IBE [30] which is a known secure scheme in the standard model with short public parameters. Because of the underlying Gentry's IBE scheme they have proved that the resulting searchable encryption scheme is also secure in the standard model, thus added a milestone to SCF_PEKS schemes.

RPS⁺: The PEKS scheme with designated tester proposed by Rhee et al. [31] adds another milestone to the secure channel-free PEKS. Here, the authors have improved the security model of the Baek et al. [27] scheme by considering a more powerful adversary. In the Baek et al. scheme, an attacker has access to trapdoors only and using those trapdoors the attacker can't get the relationship between the ciphertext and the trapdoor. However, practically an attacker may get the trapdoor of any keyword and can obtain the ciphertext related to those trapdoors provided the ciphertext is not challenge ciphertext. Secondly, the Baek et al. security model limits the attacker's capability by restricting her to share her secret key to the third party. The limitations mentioned above are addresses by Rhee et al. [31] in their scheme known as dPEKS where only a designated server chosen by the data owner is able to perform the search. The main focus is to enhance security by increasing the power of an adversary. The adversary can publish her public key without disclosing her secret key.

3.3.2.2.3 PEKS security against KGA

Searchable encryption schemes designed using public-key cryptography are likely to suffer from a KGA [32]. Because the keyword space is polynomial in size, i.e. generally a well-known set of keywords is used to perform the search, an adversary can guess the keyword corresponding to some valid captured trapdoor and generate the ciphertext for that keyword. The adversary then submits it to the cloud server to get the search result, if the search result is 1, then it signifies the guessed keyword is correct otherwise the same process is repeated again to get the information about the keyword ciphertext. In this process, the adversary gets the plaintext of the keyword, which is not expected. This process is known as the offline KGA and Byun et al. [26] launched the first successful KGA attack on the PEKS [24] scheme. After that, another attempt was made by Yau et al. [33] and they successfully launched KGA on several searchable encryption schemes based on the PKE of their time. In this section, we will discuss the efforts made in the direction to handle KGA.

Public-Key Encryption with Registered Keyword Search (PERKS): Tang and Chen [34] proposed a PERKS scheme which can handle the KGA. PERKS requires keyword registration between data owner and data user before the data owner generates the ciphertext for that keyword. For this purpose, the data user first defines a set of keywords for which the data owner can generate the ciphertext. In the keyword registration phase, the receiver (data user) will use his/her private key and the keyword to generate the pre-tag for that keyword. Now, the sender (data owner) will use this pre-tag to generate the ciphertext for that keyword, which is called the tag in this scheme. The pre-tagging mechanism makes this scheme immune to KGA. It has applications in detecting junk emails. It has a feature of aggregating any number of keyword ciphertexts into a single ciphertext. The aggregated ciphertexts have the same size as the single ciphertext. Therefore, this scheme can test multiple keyword ciphertexts in batch mode. It is the first scheme in a public-key setting which requires interaction between data owner and data user. However, this is not considered practical because every time the data user has to communicate with the data owner to retrieve desired information. Further, the data owner cannot freely choose the keywords. It also requires secure channel between the data user and the server and between the data owner and the data user.

3.3.2.2.4 SCF-PEKS with KGA security

This section will cover all those schemes which do not require a secure channel to ensure trapdoor security and are also immune to KGA.

RPS2+: The PEKS scheme with a designated tester (dPEKS) [31] suffers from KGA. This scheme was revisited by Rhee et al. [35] to make it immune to KGA. They have identified that in the previous PEKS as well as in their own dPEKS schemes, it is impossible to ensure trapdoor privacy. By capturing a valid trapdoor nothing can ever stop an attacker from guessing a keyword and generating the ciphertext for that keyword using public parameters and obtaining a test result to check if the guessed keyword is correct or not. Therefore, to ensure trapdoor privacy it is necessary to modify the structure of the trapdoor. Here, the trapdoor is generated using the public key of the server in addition to the private key of the receiver. Therefore, the trapdoor cannot disclose any information about the keyword with or without the private key of the server. They deduced that the trapdoor security implies security against KGA.

FSG2+: A PEKS variant was proposed by Fang et al. [36] proposed with the features that it did not need a secure channel and it also provided security against KGA. In earlier schemes the same goal was achieved but they needed a random oracle model to prove the security of their scheme. But this scheme was proved to be secure with a standard model. They used Gentry's IBE scheme [30] as an underlying encryption technique for the construction.

LLZ+: Recently Lu et al. [37] proposed a searchable public-key encryption using certificate-based cryptography and signcryption to provide security against KGA as well as to remove the need of a secure channel between receiver and server. This scheme does not need a secure channel and also provides security against KGA. The proposed scheme also proved to be secure in the standard model.

Table 3.3 Comparative analysis of the storage and computational cost of PEKS and its extensions

Scheme		Storage cost	Computational cost
PEKS: Boneh et al. [24]	Encrypted Index	$1\|G\| + \|\{0,1\}^{\lambda}\|$	$IP + 2E + 2H$
	Trapdoor	$1\|G\|$	$IE + IH$
	Search		$IP + IH$
Secure channel-free (SCF) PEKS			
Baek et al. [27]	Encrypted Index	$1\|G\| + \|\{0,1\}^{\lambda}\|$	$IP + IE + IE_T + 2H$
	Trapdoor	$1\|G\|$	$IE + IH$
	Search		$IP + 2E + IH$
Gu et al. [28]	Encrypted Index	$1\|G\| + \|\{0,1\}^{\lambda}\|$	$3E + 2H$
	Trapdoor	$1\|G\|$	$IE + IH$
	Search		$IP + IH$
Fang et al. [29]	Encrypted Index	$2\|G\| + 2\|G_T\|$	$3P + 3E + 3E_T + IH$
	Trapdoor	$1\|G\| + 1\|Z_p\|$	$2E$
	Search		$2P + 2E + 2E_T + IH$
Rhee et al. [31]	Encrypted Index	$1\|G\| + \|\{0,1\}^{\lambda}\|$	$7P + 2E + 2H$
	Trapdoor	$1\|G\|$	$IE + IH$
	Search		$IP + IE + IH$
PEKS secure against KGA			
Tang and Chen [34]	Encrypted Index	$1\|G\| + 1\|G_T\|$	$IP + 2E$
	Trapdoor	$1\|G\|$	$IE + IH$
	Search		IP
SCF-PEKS with KGA security			
Rhee et al. [35]	Encrypted Index	$1\|G\| + \|\{0,1\}^{\lambda}\|$	$IP + 2E + 2H$
	Trapdoor	$2\|G\|$	$3E + 2H$
	Search		$IP + 2E + 2H$
Fang et al. [36]	Encrypted Index	$\|VK\| + 1\|G_1\| + 2\|G_2\| + 2\|G_T\| + \|\sigma\|$	$3P + 8E + IH + IS$
	Trapdoor	$1\|G_1\| + 1\|Z_p\|$	IE
	Search		$4P + 2E + IE_T + IH + IV$
	Trapdoor	$1\|G\|$	$3E + 2H$
	Search		$IP + IE_T + IH$
Lu et al. [37]	Encrypted Index	$1\|G\| + \|\{0,1\}^{\lambda}\|$	$IP + 3E + IE_T + 3H$
	Trapdoor	$1\|G\|$	$3E + 2H$
	Search		$IP + IE_T + IH$

The comparative analysis of the storage and computational cost of the above discussed schemes is given in Table 3.3.

Notations used in Table 3.3 are given in Table 3.4.

The storage cost is computed in terms of size and the number of group elements. We consider the storage cost of only encryption and the trapdoor

Table 3.4 Notations used in comparative analysis along with their description

Notation	Description
$\lvert G \rvert, \lvert G_T \rvert$	Length of source (G) and target group (G_T) elements respectively in case of symmetric bilinear pairing
$\lvert G_1 \rvert, \lvert G_2 \rvert, \lvert G_T \rvert$	Length of source (G_1, G_2) and target group (G_T) elements respectively in case of asymmetric bilinear pairing
$\lvert \sigma \rvert$	Length of signature
$\lvert VK \rvert$	Length of verification key
$\lvert \{0, 1\}^{\lambda} \rvert$	Binary string of length, λ, where λ is the security parameter of the particular scheme
$\lvert Z_p \rvert$	Length of an element of a group of integers of prime order, p
$\lvert F_p \rvert$	Length of an element of a field of prime order, p
P	Bilinear pairing operation
E, E_T	Exponent operation in source and target group respectively
H	Collision resistant one-way hash function
S	Sign operation
V	Verification operation
$Poly, k$	A polynomial of degree, k

algorithm because in these algorithms we need to store their output, i.e. the ciphertext and the trapdoor at the cloud server and the user's device respectively; in the search algorithm no such cost is computed. The computational cost is computed in terms of number of operations performed by an algorithm. It is computed for the search algorithm also. There may be different types of operations performed by an algorithm like the hash operation, exponent operation, pairing operation; among them pairing is the most expensive operation. Therefore, we should try to build schemes which takes a constant number of pairing operations. If in the search algorithm we are able to make the number of pairing operations constant, then we say that the searchable encryption scheme supports fast search.

3.4 CHAPTER SUMMARY

This chapter formally introduced the concept of searchable encryption and clearly stated the need of such a technique and how this technique can be used to solve the problem of confidentiality and efficient retrieval of desired information out of the encrypted data without breaching confidentiality. We have also discussed the two broad categories of searchable encryption depending upon the underlying encryption technique and discussed the pioneering work under both the categories. Further, efforts have been made to clearly state which underlying encryption technique can provide more benefits to its users under what scenario.

REFERENCES

1. J. Wu, L. Ping, X. Ge, Y. Wang, and J. Fu, "Cloud storage as the infrastructure of cloud computing," in *2010 International Conference on Intelligent Computing and Cognitive Informatics*, 2010, pp. 380–383.
2. A. Omezzine, N. B. Ben Saoud, S. Tazi, and G. Cooperman, "Adaptive and concurrent negotiation for an efficient cloud provisioning," *Int. J. High Perform. Comput. Netw*, vol. 15, no. 3–4, pp. 145–157, 2019.
3. K. Ren, C. Wang, and Q. Wang, "Security challenges for the public cloud," *IEEE Internet Comput*, vol. 16, no. 1, pp. 69–73, 2012.
4. R.-C. Ziebell, J. Albors-Garrigos, K.-P. Schoeneberg, and M. R. P. Marin, "Adoption and success of e-HRM in a cloud computing environment: A field study," *Int. J. Cloud Appl. Comput*, vol. 9, no. 2, pp. 1–27, 2019.
5. H. Vahdat-Nejad, S. O. Eilaki, and S. Izadpanah, "Towards a better understanding of ubiquitous cloud computing," *Int. J. Cloud Appl. Comput*, vol. 8, no. 1, pp. 1–20, 2018.
6. P. Priyadarshinee, "Cloud computing adoption: Scale development, measurement and validation," *Int. J. Cloud Appl. Comput*, vol. 8, no. 1, pp. 97–116, 2018.
7. R. L. Krutz, and R. D. Vines, *Cloud Security: A Comprehensive Guide to Secure Cloud Computing*. Wiley Publishing, 2010.
8. O. O. Olakanmi, and A. Dada, "An efficient privacy-preserving approach for secure verifiable outsourced computing on untrusted platforms," *Int. J. Cloud Appl. Comput*, vol. 9, no. 2, pp. 79–98, 2019.
9. S. Kaushik, and C. Gandhi, "Ensure hierarchal identity based data security in cloud environment," *Int. J. Cloud Appl. Comput*, vol. 9, no. 4, pp. 21–36, 2019.
10. Mamta and B.B. Gupta. "An attribute-based searchable encryption scheme for non-monotonic access structure," in *Handbook of Research on Intrusion Detection Systems*, pp. 263–283. IGI Global, 2020.
11. A. Tewari, and B. B. Gupta. "An analysis of provable security frameworks for RFID security," in *Handbook of Computer Networks and Cyber Security*, pp. 635–651. Springer, Cham, 2020.
12. D. Zissis, and D. Lekkas, "Addressing cloud computing security issues," *Futur. Gener. Comput. Syst*, vol. 28, no. 3, pp. 583–592, 2012.
13. M. Zhao, H. Jiang, Z. Li, Q. Xu, H. Wang, and S. Li, "An efficient symmetric searchable encryption scheme for dynamic dataset in cloud computing paradigms," *Int. J. High Perform. Comput. Netw*, vol. 12, no. 2, pp. 179–190, 2018.
14. G. Gao, L. Wu, and Y. Yan, "A secure storage scheme with key-updating in hybrid cloud," *Int. J. High Perform. Comput. Netw*, vol. 13, no. 2, pp. 175–183, 2019.
15. D. X. Song, D. Wagner, and A. Perrig, "Practical techniques for searches on encrypted data," in *Proceeding 2000 IEEE Symposium on Security and Privacy. S&P 2000*, 2000, pp. 44–55.
16. E.-J. Goh et al., "Secure indexes," *IACR Cryptol. ePrint Arch*, Report 2003/216, http://eprint.iacr.org/2003/216.
17. Y.-C. Chang, and M. Mitzenmacher, "privacy preserving keyword searches on remote encrypted data," in *International Conference on Applied Cryptography and Network Security*, 2005, pp. 442–455.

18. R. Curtmola, J. Garay, S. Kamara, and R. Ostrovsky, "Searchable symmetric encryption: Improved definitions and efficient constructions," *J. Comput. Secur*, vol. 19, no. 5, pp. 895–934, 2011.

19. A. De Caro, and V. Iovino, "jPBC: Java pairing based cryptography," in *2011 IEEE symposium on computers and communications (ISCC)*, 2011, pp. 850–855.

20. A. Weil, "Sur les fonctions algébriquesa corps de constantes fini," *CR Acad. Sci. Paris*, vol. 210, no. 592–594, p. 149, 1940.

21. J. Tate, "WC-groups over P-ADIC fields," *Séminaire Bourbaki*, vol. 156, p. 151–156, 1957.

22. J. Tate, "Duality theorems in galois cohomology over number fields," in *Proc. Internat. Congr. Mathematicians (Stockholm, 1962)*, 1962, pp. 288–295.

23. D. Boneh, and M. Franklin, "Identity-based encryption from the Weil pairing," in *Annual international cryptology conference*, 2001, pp. 213–229.

24. D. Boneh, G. Di Crescenzo, R. Ostrovsky, and G. Persiano, "Public key encryption with keyword search," in *International conference on the theory and applications of cryptographic techniques*, 2004, pp. 506–522.

25. C. Bösch, P. Hartel, W. Jonker, and A. Peter, "A survey of provably secure searchable encryption," *ACM Comput. Surv*, vol. 47, no. 2, p. 1–51, 2014.

26. J. W. Byun, H. S. Rhee, H.-A. Park, and D. H. Lee, "Off-line keyword guessing attacks on recent keyword search schemes over encrypted data," in *Workshop on Secure Data Management*, 2006, pp. 75–83.

27. J. Baek, R. Safavi-Naini, and W. Susilo, "Public key encryption with keyword search revisited," in *International Conference on Computational Science and Its Applications*, 2008, pp. 1249–1259.

28. C. Gu, Y. Zhu, and H. Pan, "Efficient public key encryption with keyword search schemes from pairings," in *International Conference on Information Security and Cryptology*, 2007, pp. 372–383.

29. L. Fang, W. Susilo, C. Ge, and J. Wang, "A secure channel free public key encryption with keyword search scheme without random oracle," in *International Conference on Cryptology and Network Security*, 2009, pp. 248–258.

30. C. Gentry, "Practical identity-based encryption without random oracles," in *Annual International Conference on the Theory and Applications of Cryptographic Techniques*, 2006, pp. 445–464.

31. H. S. Rhee, J. H. Park, W. Susilo, and D. H. Lee, "Improved searchable public key encryption with designated tester," in *AsiaCCS*, 2009, pp. 376–379.

32. Z. Li, M. Zhao, H. Jiang, and Q. Xu, "Keyword guessing on multi-user searchable encryption," *Int. J. High Perform. Comput. Netw*, vol. 14, no. 1, p. 60–68, 2019.

33. W.-C. Yau, S.-H. Heng, and B.-M. Goi, "Off-line keyword guessing attacks on recent public key encryption with keyword search schemes," in *International Conference on Autonomic and Trusted Computing*, 2008, pp. 100–105.

34. Q. Tang, and L. Chen, "Public-key encryption with registered keyword search," in *European Public Key Infrastructure Workshop*, 2009, pp. 163–178.

35. H. S. Rhee, J. H. Park, W. Susilo, and D. H. Lee, "Trapdoor security in a searchable public-key encryption scheme with a designated tester," *J. Syst. Softw.*, vol. 83, no. 5, pp. 763–771, 2010.

36. L. Fang, W. Susilo, C. Ge, and J. Wang, "Public key encryption with keyword search secure against keyword guessing attacks without random oracle," *Inf. Sci. (Ny)*, vol. 238, p. 221–241, 2013.

37. Y. Lu, J. Li, and Y. Zhang, "Secure channel free certificate-based searchable encryption withstanding outside and inside keyword guessing attacks," *IEEE Trans. Serv. Comput.*, 2019.

Chapter 4

Introduction to provable security and its application in searchable encryption

PROVABLE SECURITY, as the name suggests, it is a type of security that can be proved. Generally, it employs mathematical proofs, and most of the security proofs are done using a reduction approach. The reduction approach used in encryption schemes is very similar to NP-completeness reductions, but more complicated. We will explain the reduction approach comprehensively manner and then present an example where we prove the security of an encryption scheme against a straightforward eavesdropper attack. With the help of examples and insights about the reductionist approach and how we can reason the security of a scheme, we can easily apply the explained approach to any system, including searchable encryption; after all, a searchable encryption scheme is also a type of encryption.

4.1 SECURITY DEFINITION

An encryption scheme is said to be complete or fully defined when, in addition to the algorithms like key generation (*Gen*), encryption (*Enc*) and decryption (*Dec*), we define all the spaces like the keyword space, message space and ciphertext space that will be implicitly used in these algorithms. Let the following represent a symmetric encryption scheme, for which we will define correctness and security definitions:

$$k \leftarrow Gen(1^n); c \leftarrow Enc(k, m); m' \leftarrow Dec(k, c)$$

The key generation algorithm takes security parameter in unary format because we want to run this algorithm in polynomial time with respect to n. The key generation algorithm implicitly uses the key space, which is a set of all the keys that can be generated by this algorithm. Similarly, the encryption and the decryption algorithms also use the ciphertext space and message space implicitly.

The correctness of an encryption scheme is defined in terms of the following probability:

$$Pr[k \leftarrow Gen(1^n); \ c \leftarrow Enc(k, m); \ m' \leftarrow Dec(k, c): m = m'] = 1 \qquad (4.1)$$

It states that we conduct an experiment where we have generated a secret key and, using this secret key, we have properly encrypted a message to get its ciphertext, and then this ciphertext is given to the decryption algorithm which also takes the same key. If the probability of getting $m = m'$ is 1, then we say our scheme is always correct. Now, we know where key and ciphertext came from, but we have not said anything about the message, where does this m came from? This m is chosen from the message space and the above defined probability must hold for all messages in the message space. Hence, we say $\forall m \in M$, if $Pr[k \leftarrow Gen(1^n); \ c \leftarrow Enc(k,m); \ m' \leftarrow Dec(k, c): m = m'] = 1$, then our scheme is always correct. Now we will define what it means for an encryption scheme to be secure.

4.1.1 Probabilistic and game-based security definition

There are many flavors of security with respect to the encryption schemes based upon the type of facilitation we have given to the adversary [1]-[3]. We define the security of the schemes against various attacks like the ciphertext-only attack, known plaintext attack (KPA), chosen plaintext attack (CPA), chosen ciphertext attack (CCA1) and adaptive chosen ciphertext attack (CCA2). In the security against ciphertext-only attack, the adversary just possesses a string of ciphertexts and tries to break the scheme using this information. In KPA, the adversary has a string of plaintext and their corresponding ciphertext. In CPA, the adversary is provided with access to the encryption oracle, and she can convert any plaintext of her choice to the ciphertext. In CCA1, in addition to the encryption oracle, the adversary has access to the decryption oracle, through which she can get the plaintext of any chosen ciphertext. In CCA2, the adversary has all the facilities that are provided to it in CCA1, but here the adversary can modify her choice based on the results of previous encryption.

To clearly understand the entire security mechanism, we will start by the security ciphertext-only attack which is also called the security against potential eavesdroppers. All further discussion in this chapter will consider the eavesdropper security.

First of all, we will define the probabilistic security definition and then convert it into the game-based definition.

Consider an experiment where we generate a secret key, k, using the *Gen* algorithm which takes security parameter, 1^n. Now, we will pass on the security parameter to the adversary and keep the key to ourselves as it is a secret. The adversary now outputs two messages, m_0, m_1 and we will allow the adversary to keep a state, which she needs later. Given these messages, we will pick a random bit, $b \leftarrow \{0, 1\}$, and encrypt one of the messages, m_b, to generate ciphertext, c, and give it back to the adversary. The adversary can now continue from the state she left and she now knows the ciphertext which we have given her. Using this information, the adversary outputs her guess, b', and wins if $b' = b$. Since b is just a single bit which can always be guessed correctly with probability $1/2$, the adversary must do more than just $1/2$, if she actually wants to break the scheme. But we do not want her to do much more than a $neg(n)$ (negligible in security parameter n) because we want our scheme to be secure. Formally, this entire experiment can be stated mathematically by the following equation, given $\forall PPT$ (probabilistic-polynomial time) adversaries, $A, \exists$ a negligible function in n, $neg(n)$, such that:

$$Pr[Gen(1^n) \rightarrow k; \; A(1^n) \rightarrow (m_0, m_1, state); \; b \leftarrow \{0, 1\}; \; Enc(k, m_b) \rightarrow c;$$
$$A(state, c) \rightarrow b': b' = b] = \frac{1}{2} + neg(n) \tag{4.2}$$

In most encryption schemes today the length of the message is not hidden in the ciphertext, therefore, the chosen message m_0, m_1 by the adversary must have equal length. Otherwise, they can be easily distinguishable.

This probabilistic security definition can also be described as a game between the challenger and the adversary as shown in Figure 4.1.

In this game between the challenger and the adversary, we say that adversary wins if $b' = b$ and we say that our scheme is secure if $\forall PPT \; A$, $\exists neg(n)$: $Pr[A \; wins \; the \; game] = \frac{1}{2} + neg(n)$. From this probability, if we subtract the trivial component, i.e. $1/2$, then what we get is technically called the advantage of adversary in winning the game, and for a scheme to be secure this advantage should be negligible.

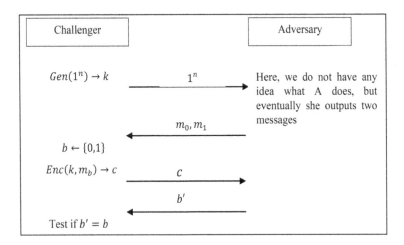

Figure 4.1 Game-based security definition.

4.2 REDUCTION PROOFS

In reduction proofs we say that a scheme X is secure as long as the assumption Y holds, where Y is a known hard assumption for which there exists no polynomial time algorithm that can break Y. We state this definition as a theorem and will provide the proof of this theorem as follows:

Theorem: If Y hold $\Rightarrow$ X is secure.

Proof: The proof methodology employed here is just like the ordinary reduction proofs, we will prove it using the contrapositive statement, which state that, if X is not secure then this should imply assumption Y should not hold.

Original: Y hold $\Rightarrow$ X secure,

Contrapositive: X is not secure $\Rightarrow$ Y does not hold

These two statements are equivalent. If we are able to prove the contrapositive, then original is automatically proved, and hence we have proved the theorem.

Potential reasoning statements: We will start the proof by assuming that if there exists a probabilistic-polynomial time (PPT) adversary, A, who can break X, then we can construct another probabilistic-polynomial time adversary, B, who can break Y. Now, here breaking entirely depends upon the security definition we have used for scheme X. For example: if eavesdropper security definition is considered, then breaking there means the adversary can distinguish between the two messages with non-negligible advantage.

An alternative way of thinking about it is, since there is no known PPT algorithm, B, that can break Y, this implies there can be no PPT algorithm, A, that can break X. If there exists some algorithm A that breaks X, then through this proof, or more appropriately reduction, we can immediately have an algorithm that breaks Y; however, if Y is a known hard assumption and no algorithm exists which can break it, then it is impossible that there can be an algorithm that can break X and thus we can claim scheme X is secure.

Since we are constructing another adversary, B, we will define its interactions and pseudocode; therefore, such a proof is also called constructive proof. All the reduction proofs work in almost the same manner, we will construct B by writing its pseudocode. B can use A as a sub-routine and the interaction of B with A is defined exactly as per the scheme X. A box diagram shown in Figure 4.2 may be useful to show the interactions clearly.

PPT algorithm B plays two key roles here, it is simulating a real challenger as A is expecting its communication with a real challenger in the security game of scheme X. On the other hand, B is acting as an adversary to the outside challenger as per the security game of scheme Y. A will receive some input from B like we have seen in the game-based security definition in Figure 4.1, but we have no idea how A works. The interesting part is to construct B and write its pseudocode such that it will simulate the challenger for A, thus its

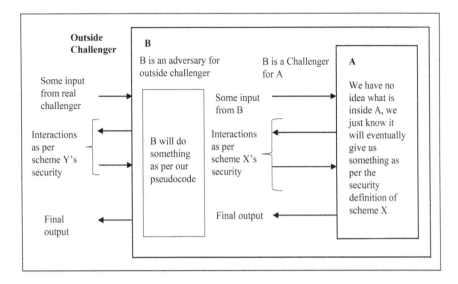

Figure 4.2 Box representation of interaction among different adversaries and the challenger in the security proof.

code should be similar to the challenger in X's security game. While writing the code, remember that B has no idea of A's working, B just knows that A is going to behave according to the security game of scheme X. If we are considering the eavesdropper security, then B knows that A will output two messages and finally it outputs a guess bit. For B, there is a different security game, the game associated with the scheme Y. Now, as far as scheme Y is concerned, we know B will behave as an adversary and will interact with some outside challenger defined for scheme Y. This outside challenger will give something to B as per the security game of scheme Y, and like A, B can also send to and receive back something from the outside challenger. Finally, B also needs to output something in order to win the security game Y. For the scheme Y, there exists a well-defined code for the challenger (outside challenger).

For scheme X, we just know the interaction between A and B and we have to write the code for B. However, for scheme Y, we know both the interaction as well as the code. Hence, our goal is to write down code for B such that the interaction with the outside challenger is somehow tied to the interaction of B with A. At the end, if A wins the security game of X, we hopefully want B to win the security game of Y.

There are three rules in a reduction approach:

- The algorithm we construct, i.e. B, must be a PPT algorithm. We have to consider three things to make sure B is a PPT algorithm. First, the pseudocode that we will write for B must take polynomial time (PT). Second, inside B, A is called as a sub-routine; we do not know the working of A, but one thing we know is whatever is done by A is done in PT. Therefore, overall, first and second together also results in PT. Third, the interactions of B with the outside challenger must be polynomial number.

- The second rule is about the simulation. B simulating the challenger for A. The interactions between A and B, as far as A is concerned, must be indistinguishable, i.e. B should do exactly the same as a real challenger would have done in the security game of X. Alternatively, we can say B's behavior in terms of the interaction with A should be like the behavior of a challenger in the security game of scheme X.

- The third rule is about the probability of winning the security game. A wins the security game X (this means correctly distinguishing the messages and thus correctly guessing the bit, in the case of eavesdropper security) with probability $1/2 + non - neg(n)$. Now, let's says B's winning condition is that it needs to find something with non-negligible advantage. Now, what we need to show is that, if A wins the security game X, then B takes the output of A and runs it through some code and outputs its response and B must also win the security game Y with non-negligible advantage.

For every reduction proof, while writing the code for B, we need to analyze these three rules.

Reasoning in terms of the contrapositive: The contrapositive of the third rule as shown in Figure 4.3 is the following: since we do not know any such algorithm B that has non-negligible advantage, therefore, all the algorithms that try to break Y have only negligible advantage, because Y is a known hard problem. As for the contrapositive, this means that all the algorithms, A, must also have the negligible advantage. Hence, the scheme X is secure.

To see the application of the reduction approach, we consider a simple pseudo-random generator (PRG)-based encryption scheme. Here, we are basically developing a practical on-time pad. As mentioned in Chapter 2, one-time pad (OTP) has perfect secrecy but it cannot be applied to messages of very long length because we have to take the same length key in order to encrypt the message.

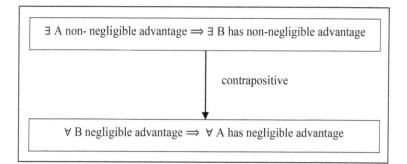

Figure 4.3 Application of contrapositive to the third rule of reduction approach.

4.2.1 Example of reduction proof

PRG is a function, G, which takes n-bit input and produces n'-bit output. It is a deterministic algorithm which produces something that looks random, but itself is not a randomized algorithm. A PRG is said to be secure if the attacker/distinguisher, D, cannot distinguish whether the output is pure random (R) or pseudorandom (PR). PRG is assumed to be secure as long as the seed, s, it initially takes is purely random. Formally, PRG security is defined in terms of the distinguishing probability.

$\forall$ PPT D, $\exists$ negligible function in security parameter, n, $neg(n)$, such that

$$Pr[s \leftarrow \{0,1\}^n; r \leftarrow G(s): D(1^n, r) \rightarrow R] - Pr[r \leftarrow \{0,1\}^{n'}: D(1^n, r) \rightarrow R] = \pm neg(n)$$
(4.3)

It signifies that the distinguisher indeed cannot distinguish between R and PR with no more than a negligible probability.

PRG-based Encryption Scheme (X):
The scheme X contains the following algorithms:

- $k \leftarrow Gen(1^n): k \leftarrow \{0,1\}^n$
- $c \leftarrow Enc(k, m): G(k) \oplus m = c$
- $m' \leftarrow Dec(k, c): G(k) \oplus c = m'$

Since $G(k)$ maps n-bit to n'-bit, therefore, message space is $\{0,1\}^{n'}$. This scheme is perfectly correct, as xoring a value with itself results in 0. The security of this scheme is proved with the help of following theorem:

Theorem: If G is a secure PRG then scheme X is a secure encryption scheme under single message eavesdropper security.

Proof: If $\exists$ PPT A who breaks X then we will construct another PPT adversary B, who breaks G. B will play the PRG security game, the challenger provides a security parameter and some value r, that may be either randomly picked or a random seed was picked by G, and computed r as a pseudorandom. Let us draw the box diagram shown in Figure 4.4, which will help us in understanding the proof clearly. As we can see in Figure 4.4, inside B we will play the security game of encryption scheme X. A is given the security parameter like B and A will give us m_0, m_1 as per the eavesdropper security definition and B will return encryption of one of these messages, m_b and send c to A. Finally, A outputs, b' as its guess for, b.

Now, we need to write the pseudocode for B, keeping in mind that B behaves like a challenger to A in X's security game and as an adversary in PRG's security game. The security parameter received from the PRG challenger is just passed on from B to A. For the encryption part, B will pick up a bit $b \leftarrow \{0,1\}$ and then it will encrypt m_b, but it will need to tie it to the random or pseudorandom value, r,

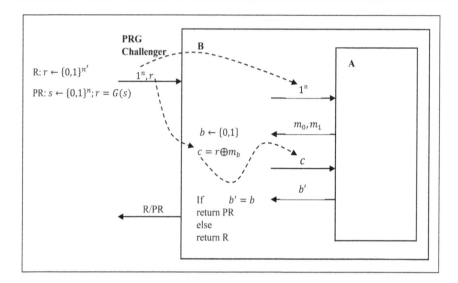

Figure 4.4 Box representation of reduction proof approach of scheme X.

in the PRG security game. Hence, B computes, $c = r \oplus m_b$ and send it to A. Now, A does something and returns b', upon receiving b', now we have two options:

- If $b' = b$, i.e. A correctly guess, then we will output pseudorandom
- Otherwise, we will output random

The reason here is that if r is pseudorandomly generated then what we are providing to A is what she is expecting, an encrypted message; then we say A breaks X with non-negligible advantage. If r was indeed random, then the given encryption scheme is an OTP, which we know is perfectly secure.

Possible reasoning: The first and second rule of the reduction proof trivially holds as we have seen in the above discussion. For the third rule, we need to first define the distinguishing probability for which we have to consider the two possible cases: first, B outputs random (R) given that indeed r was random, i.e. $Pr[B \rightarrow R|r \ is \ R]$; second, B outputs random (R) but now it is given a pseudorandom (PR), i.e. $Pr[B \rightarrow R|r \ is \ PR]$. B breaks G means the difference between these two probabilities is non-negligible.

Alternatively, we may think: when does B output R, when $b' \neq b$. So, $Pr[B \rightarrow R|r \ is \ R]$ is equivalent to $Pr[b' \neq b|r \ is \ R]$. When r is R, encryption is exactly a OTP. We know $Pr[b' \neq b] = Pr[b' = b] = \frac{1}{2}$. Also, $Pr[B \rightarrow PR|r \ is \ PR]$ is equivalent to $Pr[b' \neq b|r \ is \ PR]$ and $Pr[b' \neq b|r \ is \ PR]$ is the probability of A losing the security game X. We know the winning probability of A is $\frac{1}{2} + non-neg(n)$.

Hence, $Pr[b' \neq b | r \text{ is } PR] = \frac{1}{2} - non - neg(n)$. The distinguishing probability can now be easily calculated as $\frac{1}{2} - \left(\frac{1}{2} - non - neg(n)\right) = non - neg(n)$. Now, we will backtrack; we assumed that PRG is secure, so this distinguishing probability must be negligible and say it as $\varepsilon(n)$. So, the probability of A winning security game X is $\frac{1}{2} + \varepsilon(n)$, where $\varepsilon(n)$ is negligible. This proves if G is a secure PRG then X must be secure.

The proof approach will remain in the case of searchable encryption schemes also; what varies is the security definition and the requirements, which we will state in the next section.

4.3 COMMON SECURITY DEFINITIONS IN SEARCHABLE ENCRYPTION

The first formal security definition for searchable encryption schemes was given by Goh [4]. They introduced security definition in symmetric key setting and defined the security of searchable index as the indistinguishability of keywords against adaptive chosen keyword attack (IND1-CKA). The definition states that the adversary cannot find any information about the data file by looking at its index provided the data file must be of equal length. This is similar to what we have seen in the general security definition where we assumed the messages must be equal length; otherwise, trivially they become distinguishable. Further, they specified that IND1-CKA does not require the trapdoor to be secure because they developed their scheme to be used as a secure data structure, which can have many other applications than just SSE, and most of the applications do not require the trapdoor to be secure. Chang and Mitzenmacher [5] introduced a stronger notion of security as compared to IND1-CKA security, in the sense that equal size restriction on the size of the documents is no longer needed and they also added the notion of trapdoor security in their definition. They assumed that the size of the documents may not be equal; however, they seem to contain the same number of keywords. Indeed, more factors were considered in the definition by [5], but their security definition has a flaw in it, which is pointed by Curtmola et al. [6]: the security conditions they mentioned for a SSE to be secure are satisfied by even an insecure SSE. Later Goh revisited their security definition and enhanced IND1-CKA by relaxing the equal-size document restriction like [5] and formally called in IND2-CKA. IND2-CKA indeed protects the document size, but does not consider the security of trapdoors. After, reviewing all the prevailing security definitions, Curtmola et al. [6] remarked that it is essential to consider the security of trapdoors because of their inherent association with the security of indexes. They introduced two security definitions for searchable encryption schemes, which became the standard definitions and are still used. Formally, they called them IND-CKA1 (indistinguishability against non-adaptive chosen keyword attack) and IND-CKA2 (indistinguishability against adaptive chosen keyword attack). Both of these definitions ensured that the index as well as the search trapdoor does not reveal any information about the data file and the keywords associated with the data file. The difference between IND-CKA1 and IND-CKA2 lies in how and when the adversary can ask queries. IND-CKA1 ensures security if all the queries are asked once before the challenge phase and IND-CKA2 allows the adversary to ask queries adaptively as a function of previous queries and search result. Therefore, IND-CKA2 is considered stronger than IND-CKA1.

In the public-key setting, the first security definition for searchable encryption was given by Boneh et al. [7]. It is simply called IND-CKA, and it states that the adversary cannot get any information about the keywords until it has the trapdoor for that keyword. This security definition is similar to the eavesdropper's security; here the adversary will choose two keywords (w_0, w_1) of her choice which are encrypted by the challenger and given back to the adversary. By looking at the keyword ciphertext, the adversary cannot tell whether it is the encryption of keyword w_0 or w_1, unless it has the trapdoor for that keyword. Another famous security definition for searchable encryption in a public-key setting was proposed by Canetti et al. [8] called selective security against CKA. It is the same as IND-CKA but here the adversary has to commit the keywords it intends to attack at the beginning of the security game. These two definitions are modeled as a security game between the challenger and the adversary (basics of which were covered in Section 4.1.1). The security game consists of the following phases as shown in Figure 4.5:

Setup Phase. The challenger runs $Setup(1^n)$ algorithm. It outputs the master secret key, MSK, which is kept by him and the public parameters, PP, which are sent to the adversary.

Phase 1. In this phase, adversary can issue secret key and trapdoor queries. The challenger runs a key generation algorithm using the MSK it possesses and generates a secret key, SK. Given a keyword, w, challenger runs $Trapdoor(SK, w)$ which outputs a trapdoor, T_w. The challenger then sends T_w to adversary. The adversary can issue polynomial many queries in this phase.

Challenge Phase. Here, the adversary picks a pair $\{w_0, w_1\}$ on which it wishes to be challenged and sends them to the challenger. Given $\{w_0, w_1\}$, the challenger selects a binary bit $b \leftarrow \{0, 1\}$, and outputs C_β using the generate index algorithm and sends it to the adversary.

Phase 2. This phase is identical to Phase 1 with the condition that $\mathcal{A}$ cannot query for the trapdoor corresponding to challenge keyword $\{w_0, w_1\}$.

Output Phase/Guess Phase. Here, the adversary outputs a bit b' as its guess for b.

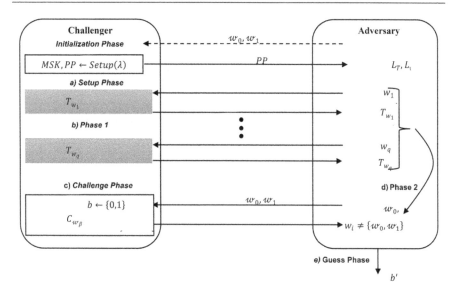

Figure 4.5 Game-based security definition for searchable encryption in public-key setting.

Let $Adv = Pr[\beta = \beta'] - \dfrac{1}{2} = \varepsilon$ be the advantage of adversary in winning the game, the searchable encryption scheme is secure if ε is negligible.

In the selective security game, in addition to these phases, we have one more phase called the initialization phase at the very beginning of the security game. In this phase, the adversary must specify the challenge keywords, $\{w_0, w_1\}$, it intends to attack. It is shown with a dashed arrow in Figure 4.5.

4.4 SECURITY/COMPLEXITY ASSUMPTIONS AND PROOF STRATEGIES

The security of searchable encryption schemes is generally proved by embedding the security assumptions into their construction. Security assumptions are well-known hard problems in cryptography. By the reduction approach we reduce our scheme to these hard problems and claim the security of the scheme by that fact that if we cannot break these hard problems then one cannot break our scheme. The security assumptions are broadly categorized into weak and strong assumptions [9]. Weak assumptions ensure security as close as to discrete logarithm (DL) assumption and are also called the standard assumptions. The computational Diffie–Hellman (CDH) assumption is an example of a weak assumption. These are referred to as weak in terms of the time it takes to break these assumptions, which is significantly higher than the strong assumptions. Hence, weak assumptions are hard to break as compared to strong assumptions. Strong assumptions are those assumptions whose security levels are lower as compared to the DL assumption. Strong assumptions are relatively risky and unreliable [9]. The commonly used security assumptions in literature for developing searchable encryption schemes are given in Table 4.1.

Table 4.1 Commonly used security assumption in the construction of searchable encryption schemes

S.No.	Security assumption	Description
1.	Discrete Logarithm (DL) Assumption	Given $h \in G$, it is hard to find x: $h = g^x$ [10].
2.	Computational Diffie–Hellman (CDH) Assumption	Given $g^x \in G$ and $g^y \in G$, it is hard to find g^{xy} [11].
3.	Decision Diffie–Hellman (DDH) Assumption	Given $g^x \in G$, $g^y \in G$ and $h \in G$, it is hard to determine if $h = g^{xy}$ or not. [12].
4.	Parallel Decisional Diffie–Hellman (pDDH) Assumption	Given $g^{x_1}, g^{x_2}, \cdots, g^{x_n}, h_1, h_2, \cdots, h_n \in G$, it is hard to determine if $h_1 = g^{x_1 x_2}$, $h_2 = g^{x_2 x_3}$, $\cdots$, $h_{n-1} = g^{x_{n-1} x_n}$, $h_n = g^{x_n x_1}$ or not [12].
5.	q-Diffie–Hellman Inversion (q-DHI) Assumption	Given $g^x, g^{x^2}, \cdots, g^{x^q} \in G$, it is hard to compute $g^{\frac{1}{x}}$ [13], [14].
6.	q-Decision Diffie–Hellman Inversion (q-DDHI) Assumption	Given $g^x, g^{x^2}, \cdots, g^{x^q}, h \in G$, it is hard to determine if $h = g^{\frac{1}{x}}$ [13].
7.	Linear Assumption	Given $g^u, g^v, g^{xu}, g^{yv} \in G$; it is hard to find $g^{x+y} \in G$ [15].
8.	q-Linear Assumption	Let $g_1, g_2, \cdots, g_q, g_0$ be the generators of group G. Given $g_1, g_2, \cdots, g_q, g_0, g_1^{x_1}, g_2^{x_2}, \cdots, g_q^{x_q} \in G$; it is hard to find $g_0^{x_0}$ where $x_0 = \sum_{i=1}^{q} x_i$ [15].
9.	Decision Linear (DLIN) Assumption	Given $g^u, g^v, g^{xu}, g^{yv}, h \in G$; it is hard to determine if $h = g^{x+y}$. This assumption is used in place of DDH particularly in Bilinear groups where DDH is no more a hard assumption [15].
10.	q-Decision Linear (q-DLIN) Assumption	Let $g_1, g_2, \cdots, g_q, g_{q+1}$ be the generators of group G. Given $g_1, g_2, \cdots, g_q, g_{q+1}, g_1^{x_1}, g_2^{x_2}, \cdots, g_q^{x_q}, h \in G$; it is hard to determine if $h = g_{q+1}^{\sum_{i=1}^{q} x_i}$ [15].
11.	q-Strong Diffie–Hellman (q-SDH) Assumption	Given $g^x, g^{x^2}, \cdots, g^{x^q} \in G$, it is hard to find $u \in Z_p$ and $g^{\frac{1}{x+u}}$ [13].
12.	Diffie–Hellman Exponent (DHE) Assumption	Given $g_0, g_1, g_2, \cdots, g_q, g_{q+2}, \cdots, g_{2q} \in G$, where $g_i\big|_{1 \le i \le 2q,\, i \ne q+1} = g^{x^i}$, it is hard to find $g_{q+1} = g^{x^{q+1}}$ [16].
13.	Hash Diffie–Hellman (HDH) Assumption	Let $H: \{0,1\}^* \rightarrow \{0,1\}^{len}$ be a hash function which returns a binary string of length say len. Given $g, g^x, g^y, H(g^{xy}), Z = \{0,1\}^{len}$; it is hard to find if $Z = H(g^{xy})$ [17].

(Continued)

Table 4.1 (Continued)

S.No.	Security Assumption	Description
14.	Symmetric External Diffie–Hellman (SXDH) Assumption	Let $e: G_1 \times G_2 \to G_T$ be an asymmetric bilinear map between G_1 and G_2. Let $j \in \{1, 2\}$ and g_j be the generator of G_j. Given $g_j^x, g_j^y, g_j^{xy}, h_j \in G_j$, it is hard to determine if $h_j = g_j^{xy}$ [18]. It signifies that DDH is hard in both the groups.
15.	Knowledge of Exponents Assumption (KEA)	If on input g and g^x $\mathcal{A}$ ouputs (Z, C): $C = Z^x$ then there exists an extractor which on same input returns z: $g^z = Z$ [19].
16.	Bilinear Diffie–Hellman (BDH) Assumption	Given g, g^x, g^y and $g^z \in G$, it is hard to find $e(g, g)^{xyz}$ [20].
17.	Decision Bilinear Diffie–Hellman (DBDH) Assumption	Given $g, g^x, g^y, g^z \in G$ and $X \in G_T$, it is hard to determine if $X = e(g, g)^{xyz}$ [20].
18.	Modified Decisional Diffie–Hellman (MDDH) Assumption	This assumption is based on DBDH assumption. Given $g, g^x, g^y, g^z, g^{xyz} \in G$ and $X \in G$, it is hard to determine if $X = g^{xyz}$ [21].
19.	Bilinear Decision Linear (BDLIN) Assumption	Given $G, G_T, e, \{g_1, g_2, g_1^x, g_2^y \in G\}, X \in G_T : x, y, z \in Z_p$, it is hard to determine if $X = e(g_1, g_2)^{x+y}$ [22].
20.	q-Bilinear Diffie–Hellman Inversion (q-BDHI) Assumption	Given $G, G_T, e, \{g_i^x, g_i^{x^2}, \ldots, g_i^{x^q}\}_{i \in \{1, 2\}}$, it is hard to find $e(g_1, g_2)^{\frac{1}{x}}$ [23].
21.	q-Decision Bilinear Diffie–Hellman Inversion (q-DBDHI) Assumption	Given $G, G_T, e, \{g_i^x, g_i^{x^2}, \ldots, g_i^{x^q}\}_{i \in \{1, 2\}}, X \in G_T$, it is hard to determine if $X = e(g_1, g_2)^{\frac{1}{x}}$ [24].
22.	q-weak Bilinear Diffie–Hellman Inversion (q-wBDHI) Assumption	Given $G, G_T, e, \{g_i^x, g_i^{x^2}, \ldots, g_i^{x^q}, g_i^y\}_{i \in \{1, 2\}}$, it is hard to find $e(g_1, g_2)^{x^{q+1}y}$ [24].
23.	q-weak Bilinear Decision Diffie–Hellman Inversion (q-wDBDHI) Assumption	Given $G, G_T, e, \{g_i^x, g_i^{x^2}, \ldots, g_i^{x^q}, g_i^y\}_{i \in \{1, 2\}} X \in G_T$, it is hard to determine if $X = e(g_1, g_2)^{x^{q+1}y}$ [24].
24.	Multi-Sequence of Exponents Diffie–Hellman (MSEDH) Assumption	Given $e: G_1 \times G_2 \to G_T, g_0, h_0$ be the generators of group G_1, G_2 respectively, l, m, t be three integers and f, g be two co-prime polynomials of order l, m respectively and the following exponentiations: $$g_0, g_0^\alpha, \ldots, g_0^{\alpha^{l+t-2}}, g_0^{k\gamma f(\alpha)};$$ $$g_0^\gamma, g_0^{\alpha\gamma}, \ldots, g_0^{\gamma \alpha^{l+t}};$$ $$h_0, h_0^\alpha, \ldots, h_0^{\alpha^{m-2}};$$ $$h_0^\gamma, h_0^{\alpha\gamma}, \ldots, h_0^{\gamma \alpha^{2m-1}};$$ $$h_0^{kg(\alpha)}, T \in G_T$$ It is hard to decide if $T = e(g_0, h_0)^{kf(\alpha)}$ [25].
25.	Truncated decisional augmented Bilinear Diffie–Hellman (q-ABDHE) Assumption	Given $g, g^x, g^{x^2}, \cdots, g^{x^q}, g^{zx}, g^{zx^{q+2}} \in G$ and $e(g, g)^{zx^{q+1}}, X \in G_T$ where $x, z \in Z_p$, it is hard to determine if $X = e(g, g)^{zx^{q+1}}$ [26].

In the above table, G refers to the cyclic group of prime order p with generator g; and $e: G_1 \times G_2 \to G_T$, refers to the asymmetric bilinear map from the source group G_1 and G_2 to the target group G_T, where both G_1 and G_2 are cyclic groups of prime order p such that g_1, g_2 be the generator of G_1 and G_2 respectively and $e(g, g)$ be the generator of G_T.

4.4.1 Random oracle model and standard model

Most of the encryption schemes including the searchable encryption are proved secure in either the random oracle model or the standard model. These are considered as both the design as well as the proof strategies. In the standard model, the only constraint on the adversary that it considers is of the computational resources i.e. the time and the computational power, and therefore it is also called the computational model. In the standard model only security/complexity assumptions are used to prove the security of a scheme. In the random oracle model, apart from the security assumptions, one more assumption is made about the cryptographic primitives. It considers them as ideal primitives; for example, the cryptographic hashes in the random oracle model are considered as a pure random function. It is efficient and relatively easy to prove the scheme in the random oracle model, but the practitioners focus more on developing the scheme using the standard model because when these idealized primitives are replaced with the actual ones, it may not guarantee the security of the scheme in the practical scenarios.

4.5 CHAPTER SUMMARY

This chapter introduced the concept of provable security and its application in developing a secure searchable encryption. This chapter provided the basic security definitions used in searchable encryption and also explains the different security models that can be employed to prove the security of a searchable encryption scheme. Moreover, this chapter provided an introduction to cryptographic assumptions used in provable security and cited the commonly used assumptions in searchable encryption.

REFERENCES

1. Z. Yu, C. Z. Gao, Z. Jing, B. B. Gupta, and Q. Cai, "A practical public key encryption scheme based on learning parity with noise," *IEEE Access*, vol. 6, pp. 31918–31923, 2018.
2. C. Yu, J. Li, X. Li, X. Ren, and B. B. Gupta, "Four-image encryption scheme based on quaternion Fresnel transform, chaos and computer generated hologram," *Multimedia Tools and Applications*, vol. 77, no. 4, pp. 4585–4608, 2018.

3. X. Wang, Y. Zhang, B. B. Gupta, H. Zhu, and D. Liu, "An identity-based signcryption on lattice without trapdoor," *J. UCS*, vol. 25, no. 3, pp. 282–293, 2019.

4. E.-J. Goh et al., "Secure indexes," *IACR Cryptol. ePrint Arch*, Report 2003/216, http://eprint.iacr.org/2003/216.

5. Y.-C. Chang, and M. Mitzenmacher, "privacy preserving keyword searches on remote encrypted data," in *International Conference on Applied Cryptography and Network Security*, 2005, pp. 442–455.

6. R. Curtmola, J. Garay, S. Kamara, and R. Ostrovsky, "Searchable symmetric encryption: Improved definitions and efficient constructions,", *J. Comput. Secur*, vol. 19, no. 5, pp. 895–934, 2011.

7. D. Boneh, G. Di Crescenzo, R. Ostrovsky, and G. Persiano, "Public key encryption with keyword search," in *International Conference on the Theory and Applications of Cryptographic Techniques*, 2004, pp. 506–522.

8. R. Canetti, S. Halevi, and J. Katz, "A forward-secure public-key encryption scheme," in *International Conference on the Theory and Applications of Cryptographic Techniques*, 2003, pp. 255–271.

9. F. Guo, W. Susilo, and Y. Mu, *Introduction to Security Reduction*. Springer Cham, Switzerland, 2018, https://doi.org/10.1007/978-3-319-93049-7.

10. C.-P. Schnorr, "Efficient signature generation by smart cards,", *J. Cryptol*, vol. 4, no. 3, pp. 161–174, 1991.

11. D. Boneh, and R. J. Lipton, "Algorithms for black-box fields and their application to cryptography," in *Annual International Cryptology Conference*, 1996, pp. 283–297.

12. D. Boneh, "The Decision Diffie-Hellman problem," *In: Buhler J.P. (eds) Algorithmic Number Theory. ANTS 1998. Lecture Notes in Computer Science*, vol 1423. Springer, Berlin, Heidelberg. https://doi.org/10.1007/BFb0054851, 1998.

13. D. Boneh, and X. Boyen, "Short signatures without random oracles and the SDH assumption in bilinear groups,", *J. Cryptol*, vol. 21, no. 2, pp. 149–177, 2008.

14. B. Libert, and J.-J. Quisquater, "Improved signcryption from q-Diffie-Hellman problems," in *International Conference on Security in Communication Networks*, 2004, pp. 220–234.

15. D. Boneh, X. Boyen, and H. Shacham, "Short group signatures," in *Annual International Cryptology Conference*, 2004, pp. 41–55.

16. C. Delerablée, "Identity-based broadcast encryption with constant size ciphertexts and private keys," in *International Conference on the Theory and Application of Cryptology and Information Security*, 2007, pp. 200–215.

17. M. Abdalla, M. Bellare, and P. Rogaway, "DHAES: An encryption scheme based on the Diffie-Hellman problem.," Cryptology ePrint Archive, Report 1999/007, https://eprint.iacr.org/1999/007.

18. J. Groth, and A. Sahai, "Efficient non-interactive proof systems for bilinear groups," in *Annual International Conference on the Theory and Applications of Cryptographic Techniques*, 2008, pp. 415–432.

19. M. Bellare, and A. Palacio, "The knowledge-of-exponent assumptions and 3-round zero-knowledge protocols," in *Annual International Cryptology Conference*, 2004, pp. 273–289.

20. D. Boneh, and M. Franklin, "Identity-based encryption from the Weil pairing," in *Annual International Cryptology Conference*, 2001, pp. 213–229.

21. M. H. Ameri, M. Delavar, J. Mohajeri, and M. Salmasizadeh, "A key-policy attribute-based temporary keyword search scheme for secure cloud storage," *IEEE Trans. Cloud Comput.*, vol. 8, no. 3, pp. 660–671, 2020, https://doi.org/10.1109/TCC.2018.2825983.

22. M. Backes, D. Fiore, and R. M. Reischuk, "Verifiable delegation of computation on outsourced data," in *Proceedings of the 2013 ACM SIGSAC Conference on Computer & Communications Security*, 2013, pp. 863–874.

23. D. Boneh, and X. Boyen, "Efficient selective-ID secure identity-based encryption without random oracles," in *International Conference on the Theory and Applications of Cryptographic Techniques*, 2004, pp. 223–238.

24. D. Boneh, X. Boyen, and E.-J. Goh, "Hierarchical identity based encryption with constant size ciphertext," in *Annual International Conference on the Theory and Applications of Cryptographic Techniques*, 2005, pp. 440–456.

25. C. Delerablée, and D. Pointcheval, "Dynamic threshold public-key encryption," in *Annual International Cryptology Conference*, 2008, pp. 317–334.

26. C. Gentry, "Practical identity-based encryption without random oracles," in *Annual International Conference on the Theory and Applications of Cryptographic Techniques*, 2006, pp. 445–464.

Chapter 5

Searchable encryption in a public-key setting

SEARCHABLE ENCRYPTION IN A PUBLIC-KEY SETTING provides flexibility as there is no need of complicated secret key-sharing processes among the users as compared to the symmetric-key setting, which makes it suitable for the multi-user shared cloud storage environment. Cloud storage is becoming very popular among organizations because of features like optimized storage cost, ease of data management, and anytime anywhere access capabilities, and slowly cloud storage is becoming a necessity. However, organizations feel somewhat reluctant to adopt this platform because of security concerns. The data stored at the third-party cloud server may not be safe if it is stored as it is in plaintext form. To resolve the trust issues, it is suggested to store the data in encrypted form. This solves the problem; however, the selective access of the data becomes infeasible. One trivial solution is to first download all the data and decrypt it locally, but in that case, why would someone use cloud storage, if everything has to be done manually? The user must be able to retrieve only the desired data from the encrypted data stored at the cloud server. The first requirement to retrieve the desired data is the ability to perform a search over the encrypted data. A searchable encryption technique plays a critical role in this scenario. As we know, searchable encryption can be developed using either the symmetric-key or the public-key setting. Using a symmetric-key setting to create the searchable encryption scheme for the shared cloud storage environment may cause a lot of complexity in terms of sharing the secret key among the cloud users. As the number of users increases, the internal secret key distribution process also becomes difficult. Therefore, the public-key setting is preferred. In this chapter, we will discuss all aspects of the searchable encryption scheme in a public-key setting.

5.1 SYSTEM DEFINITION AND SYSTEM MODEL

In this section, we will formally define searchable encryption by introducing the different algorithms involved in a searchable encryption scheme and also provide the correctness condition for the searchable encryption schemes using the probabilistic definitions given in Chapter 4. Further, we will discuss the architecture of a searchable encryption system and explain the role of each entity involved in the system.

5.1.1 System definition

Like any encryption scheme, the searchable encryption scheme also consists of the four basic algorithms: key generation, index generation, trapdoor generation, and search. These algorithms are derived from the algorithms in an encryption scheme, and we will discuss the similarity and relationship between each algorithm here and the algorithms in any standard public-key encryption (PKE) scheme.

- $[K_{pub}, K_{pri}] \leftarrow GenKey(1^n)$: The key-generation algorithm here and in any standard PKE scheme are the same. This algorithm also takes the security parameter (unary format) and outputs the public and private key pairs, like any PKE scheme.
- $C_j \leftarrow GenIndex(K_{pub}, w_j)$: The index-generation algorithm is the same as the encryption algorithm in any PKE scheme. It also takes the public key and encrypts the keywords associated with the data file using this public key. Usually, in a PKE scheme, we encrypt a message with the public key, here the message is equivalent to the keyword. The collection of ciphertext of the keyword is sometimes called the encrypted index because, by default, the direct or the inverted index approach is implemented by the cloud server to store the encrypted data files and their associated encrypted keywords. Thus, in the context of searchable encryption this algorithm is called the index-generation algorithm; otherwise, it is merely an encryption algorithm.
- $T_i \leftarrow GenTrap(K_{pri}, w_i)$: The trapdoor-generation algorithm is similar to the decryption algorithm in a PKE scheme in terms of one input, i.e., the private key of the user. But instead of taking the ciphertext at this step, a searchable encryption scheme conserves it for the search step. Typically, the secret key is used for decryption, but here we want to delegate our search capability to the cloud server using this secret key but without disclosing it. Here, for each keyword we want to search, we generate a kind of secret key for that keyword, and in the cryptographic community, it is called the search trapdoor or sometimes the search token. The search trapdoor, just like a usual computer trapdoor, facilitates the cloud server performing a search over the encrypted data.
- $0/1 \leftarrow Search(T_i, C_j)$: The search algorithm is a new algorithm concerning PKE schemes. This algorithm uses the trapdoor of the keyword and searches each ciphertext for that keyword. If a match is found it returns 1, otherwise it returns 0. Sometimes it is explicitly shown in a scheme

that it returns a reference of the data file associated with that keyword; otherwise, it is implicitly assumed that the associated data files will be provided to the user who generated the trapdoor.

$$Pr[[K_{pub}, K_{pri}] \leftarrow Genkey(1^n); C \leftarrow GenIndex(K_{pub}, w);$$
$$T \leftarrow GenTrap(K_{pri}, w): 1 \leftarrow Search(T, C)] = 1 \tag{5.1}$$

Equation 5.1 states that we conduct an experiment where we have generated a public-private key pair, and using the public key, we have appropriately encrypted a keyword to get its ciphertext, and using the corresponding private key, we generated the trapdoor for the same keyword. After that, we provided both the ciphertext and search trapdoor to the search algorithm. If the search algorithm returns binary value 1 with probability one, then we say our scheme is always correct.

This a comprehensive system definition that we have discussed; however, in the literature there exist some variants of this definition depending upon the type of method and underlying technique used for developing the searchable encryption scheme. The searchable encryption schemes may either be designed using the core of the underlying encryption scheme (like we have just discussed above) or may use a transformation method that converts the underlying encryption scheme into the searchable encryption. The system definition of a searchable encryption scheme developed using the transformation method is stated as follows:

$[PK_{SE}, SK_{SE}] \leftarrow GenKey(1^n, \mathcal{W})$: This algorithm appears similar to the key-generation algorithm stated above. But here an additional parameter, keyword space, is also taken as input. The keyword space is used to map it to the identity space (if an identity-based encryption (IBE) scheme is used as an underlying scheme) or to the attribute space (if an attribute-based encryption (ABE) scheme is used as an underlying scheme). This algorithm just runs the setup algorithm of the underlying encryption scheme with suitable mapping. The public parameters, PP, of the underlying encryption schemes are used as the public key of the searchable encryption scheme, PK_{SE} (it may include some other parameters also in addition to public parameters of the underlying encryption scheme, for example the hashes defined for mapping purpose), and the master secret key, MSK, is used as the corresponding secret key in the searchable encryption scheme, SK_{SE}.

$T_i \leftarrow GenTrap(SK_{SE}, w_i)$: This algorithm internally calls the key-generation algorithm of the underlying encryption scheme; the keyword is taken as input after mapping through some hash function. For example: if IBE is used as an underlying scheme, then a hash function, H, is used which maps each keyword with a unique identity in the identity space, $T_i \leftarrow GenKey(MSK_{IBE}, H(w_i))$.

$C_i \leftarrow GenIndex(PK_{SE}, w_i)$: This algorithm internally calls the encryption algorithm of the underlying encryption scheme. Taking the same example of an IBE scheme, this algorithms call $Enc(PP_{IBE}, H(w_i), m_i)$ the algorithm which takes the keyword after application of a hash function (maps keyword to identity) and randomly selects a message, m_i, to encrypt.

$0/1 \leftarrow Search(PK_{SE}, T_i, C_i)$: This algorithm internally calls the decryption algorithm of the underlying scheme. Taking the same example of an IBE scheme, this algorithms calls $Dec(PP_{IBE}, T_i, C_i)$ and outputs binary value 1 if the decryption algorithm correctly outputs the encrypted message, m_i; otherwise, it returns 0.

The above-stated steps present the variation of the searchable encryption definition based on the type of methodology used for developing a searchable encryption scheme. Next, we will discuss another variation depending upon the type of underlying scheme used. Here, we will consider that ABE is used as an underlying scheme and discuss the definition of the corresponding searchable encryption scheme concerning ABE. For joint presentation, let I_K denote the input to the key-generation algorithm, $GenKey$ and I_E denotes the input to the generate index algorithm, $GenIndex$. In KP-ABE, I_K and I_E are the access policy and the set of attributes, respectively. In CP-ABE, I_K and I_E are the set of attributes and the access policy, respectively.

$(PP, MSK) \leftarrow Setup(1^n, W, Att)$: The setup algorithm takes the attribute universe, $Att = \{att_1, att_2, \cdots, att_{|Att|}\}$ and keyword space, $W = \{w_1, w_2, \cdots, w_{|W|}\}$, in addition to the security parameter, 1^n, and outputs the public parameters, PP, and master secret key, MSK.

$SK_u \leftarrow GenKey(PP, MSK, I_K)$: This algorithm takes the MSK and the credentials of a user, u, I_K, and generates his private key corresponding to his credentials, i.e. SK_u.

$C_i \leftarrow GenIndex(PP, w_i \in W, I_E)$: This algorithm encrypts the keyword, w_i, using I_E and PP and outputs the ciphertext, C_i.

$T_i \leftarrow GenTrap(SK_u, w_i \in W)$: This algorithm generates the trapdoor for the keyword, w_i, using the secret key of the user u, SK_u.

$0/1 \leftarrow Search(PP, C_i, T_i)$: This algorithm will be executed only if the satisfiability condition holds between I_K and I_E. If the satisfiability condition holds, this algorithm searches for the keyword contained in the trapdoor by searching all the ciphertexts one by one and returns 1 if a match is found, otherwise it returns 0

5.1.2 System model

In a searchable encryption system there are different entities involved, and each entity executes one of the algorithms explained above in the system definition. The description of these entities, along with their role, is generally called the system model, and is shown below in Figure 5.1.

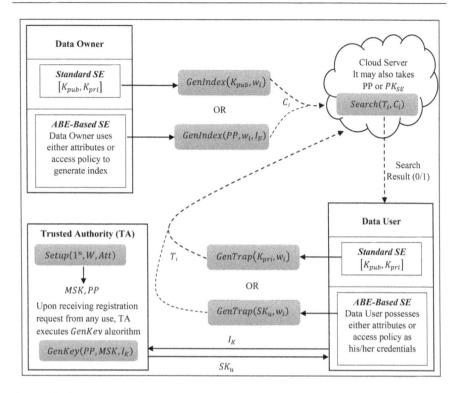

Figure 5.1 General system model for SE in PKE setting.

If a standard searchable encryption scheme is used, then we assume that each cloud user possesses a public and private secret key pair, $[K_{pub}, K_{pri}]$, generated by the key-generation center; these may be completely random keys with no relation to a person's identity or the credentials of a user as in IBE- or ABE-based SE schemes. If an IBE or ABE scheme is used as an underlying scheme, then in the key generation the information related to one's identity or credentials (attributes/access policy) is taken to generate the secret key of the user. In Figure 5.1, we have shown the system model for standard SE or SE based on ABE in a single diagram, which is explained as follows:

Trusted Authority: The trusted authority (TA) is an entity that plays its role when ABE is used as an underlying scheme to develop the searchable encryption scheme. When some new user reaches the TA for registration, the TA will verify his/her credentials and generate his/her secret key using the *GenKey* algorithm. This algorithm embeds either the access policy (KP-ABE) or the attributes (CP-ABE) associated with that user. The TA also initializes the system by executing the *Setup* algorithm, which generates the public parameters, *PP*, and the master secret key, *MSK*, out of which *PP* are made available to every cloud user.

Data Owner: The data owner (DO) is an entity that wants to share his/her data to multiple users. The DO first encrypts the data and the associated keywords by invoking the *GenIndex* algorithm. This algorithm encrypts the keyword, w_i, using K_{pub}, if a standard SE is used; otherwise, if say, ABE is used, this algorithm encrypts the keyword, w_i, using *PP* as well as the access policy (if CP-ABE is used) or the attributes (if KP-ABE is used). The data owner then uploads the encrypted data to the cloud server.

Data User: The *Data User* (DU) is an entity that wants to retrieve the data stored by the data owners at the cloud server. Since the data is in an encrypted form and DU wants the cloud server to perform a search on the encrypted data, so, the data owner must delegate his/her searching functionality to the cloud server. The data owner generates the search trapdoor using his/her secret key by executing the *GenTrap* algorithm.

Cloud Server: The cloud server (CU) is owned by a third party to provide services like storage. It stores the encrypted data and performs a search on this data using the search trapdoor supplied by the DU. If a standard SE is used, then the search algorithm takes only the ciphertext and the trapdoor for the keyword; otherwise, it may additionally requirethe *PP*, if an ABE scheme is used, or PK_{SE}, if some transformation method is used. PK_{SE} denotes the public key of the transformed searchable encryption scheme.

5.1.3 Flow of information between different parties involved in an SE system

The flow of information between different parties in an IBE-based SE system is explained in the following steps as shown in Figure 5.2. *i*) The DO sends data along with the associated keywords in an encrypted form under

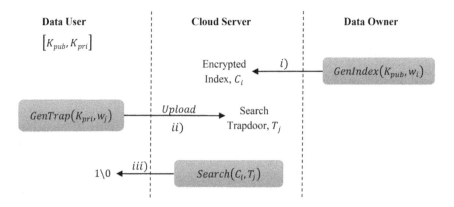

Figure 5.2 Flow of information in an IBE-based SE system.

the public key of recipient, K_{pub} using the $GenIndex(K_{pub}, w_i)$ algorithm. The resulting encrypted data along with its index is stored at the remote server for sharing it with other users. *ii*) The DU generates the trapdoor for the keyword which is associated with that particular file using the $GenTrap(K_{pri}, w_i)$ algorithm. The generated trapdoor will enable the cloud server to perform search if it is generated by the user for whom the data is intended, i.e. the trapdoor is generated using the private key of the same user whose public key was used to generate the index. *iii*) The CS performs the search over encrypted data, C_i, using the search trapdoor, T_j, sent by the DU. The search operation is done by the cloud server on the behalf of DU using the $Search(C_i, T_j)$ algorithm. If the keyword corresponding to the search trapdoor is found then the cloud server returns binary output 1; otherwise, it outputs 0.

The flow of information between different parties in an ABE-based SE system is explained in the following steps as shown in Figure 5.3.: *i*) The TA initializes the system using the $Setup(\lambda)$ algorithm which takes security parameter λ as input. Also, it issues the essential credentials to the cloud users using $KeyGen(MSK)$ algorithm which takes the master secret key as input. *ii*) A data owner is the one who would like to outsource their collection of data along with some keywords to the cloud server for the purpose of sharing. Owing to the confidential nature of the data, it is stored in an encrypted form. To upload the data over the cloud server, the data owner uses $GenIndex(PP, w_i)$ which takes public parameters, PP, and the metadata item, w_i, associated with the data file as input and generates the ciphertext, C_i of w_i. Once the data is uploaded to the cloud server, now it can be searched by the authorized users. *iii*) A DU is the one who wants to retrieve the data stored by the data owner at the cloud server. If the user is authorized, then he/she can generate a trapdoor for the keyword associated with the data file and give it to the cloud server to perform search. Suppose a DU wants to retrieve a data file which contains a particular keyword, w_j. The DU will first generate the search trapdoor/token using his secret credentials to run $GenTrap(SK_u, w_j)$ and then send the trapdoor, T_j, to the cloud server. *iv*) A cloud server stores the encrypted data and performs search operation on the behalf of the DU. The cloud server is assumed to be honest, i.e. it correctly executes the search algorithm. Upon reception of the search trapdoor/token the cloud server will perform search the encrypted data stored over it using $Search(C_i, T_j)$. If the search trapdoor/token is generated by an authorized user having valid secret credentials, then the public component in the ciphertext and the corresponding secret components in the search trapdoor/token will get cancelled out as per the rule of an encryption system. Therefore, an equality condition will hold if the keyword in the ciphertext and the search trapdoor/token matches. In such a scenario, it is said that the keyword being searched is found and therefore a binary value 1 is returned as output. Otherwise, 0 is returned which signifies that the keyword is not found. In another situation, if the search trapdoor/token is not generated by the authorized user then the search

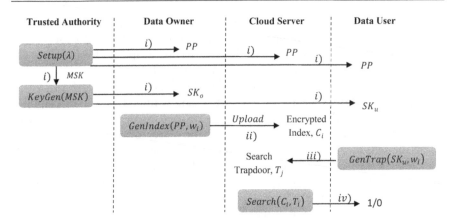

Figure 5.3 Flow of information in ABE-based SE system.

process will terminate and $\perp$ (null) is returned to the user. It signifies that the user has no right to perform search over the encrypted data shared by data owner over common storage managed by some remote cloud server.

During the entire process in both the models, the cloud server is assumed to be honest and will correctly execute all the algorithms but it may be curious to find some relevant information. Therefore, while developing a searchable encryption scheme we must ensure that the cloud server will not get any information about the plaintext of the keyword being searched. This model is known as security against chosen keyword attack (CKA) which is formally introduced in the next section.

5.2 BROAD CATEGORIES OF SEARCHABLE ENCRYPTION IN A PUBLIC-KEY SETTING

In this section, we will discuss different categories of SE schemes based on the type of underlying encryption scheme used to develop the searchable encryption schemes [1]. In public-key setting there are some leading techniques like IBE [2, [3]4], ABE [57], hidden vector encryption (HVE) etc. which are frequently used for the construction of searchable encryption scheme. Among these, we will discuss the searchable encryption schemes using the first two primitives, i.e. IBE and ABE.

5.2.1 IBE-based SE schemes

The first IBE-based searchable encryption scheme was developed by Boneh et al [8]; a detailed description of this scheme and some of its variants has already been given in Chapter 3. In this section, we will discuss the searchable

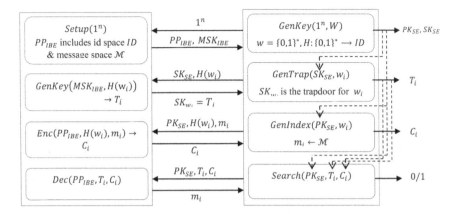

Figure 5.4 Transformation mechanism from IBE to searchable encryption.

encryption schemes developed using a transformation from the IBE scheme. The general transformation mechanism from an IBE to searchable encryption is shown below in Figure 5.4.

The first searchable encryption using the transformation method was proposed by Khader [9]. A transformation method was applied on a k-resilient IBE [2] scheme to construct the PEKS scheme. They remarked on some facts about the transformation mechanism, such as the IBE scheme which we are planning to transform to IBE must be anonymous, otherwise it would expose the keywords. Another fact concerns the consistency of the resulting SE scheme; they stated that the underlying scheme must be secure in the appropriate security model, because only then would the resulting scheme be consistent and secure. The proposed scheme is consistent because the underlying IBE scheme is secure against chosen ciphertext attack. Further, they performed multi-keyword search and also eliminated the need for the secure channel.

5.2.1.1 PEKS revisited

A formalization of the transformation mechanism from anonymous IBE to PEKS scheme was given by Abdalla et al. [10]. They formally proved the consistency of the resulting scheme. Further, they proposed the following extensions to the basic idea: *i)* added a HIBE (anonymous hierarchical IBE) to the searchable encryption transformation, and *ii)* added the concept of temporary keyword search. The temporary keyword search prevents the server from learning about the past and future keyword ciphertexts once the server has received the trapdoor. Hence, even if the server memorizes the trapdoor it cannot find the link between the trapdoor and the keyword ciphertext. This was achieved by limiting the duration for which the trapdoor is valid.

5.2.1.2 PEFKS

An instantiation of the transformation mechanism was first given by Xu et al [11]. For demonstration purposes they have used an IBE scheme by Boneh and Franklin [12]. Further, they have developed a method to make their scheme immune to KGA. In their method, they divided the trapdoor into fuzzy and exact trapdoors such that two or more keywords share the same fuzzy trapdoor. When the receiver wanted to search something then he/she would send the fuzzy trapdoor to the cloud server. The cloud server could not guess the keyword even if had the fuzzy trapdoor for all the keywords, which resulted in a scheme which was immune to KGA. To construct the fuzzy trapdoor, they used a fuzzy function which returned the same fuzzy value for every two keywords if the keyword space was even. If the keyword space was odd, then the last three keywords had the same fuzzy value and for the rest of the keywords every two keywords had the same fuzzy value. Therefore, with a probability of $1/2$ or $1/3$ the malicious cloud server could still guess the keyword associated with the search trapdoor. Hence, to a make a scheme more secure against KGA there is a need to further reduce this probability and this was achieved by designing a fuzzy function which used the modulus operator and the concept of congruence class [13]. They designed their fuzzy function such that k keywords share the same fuzzy trapdoor, thus reduced the keyword guessing probability to $1/k$ and hence improved the security against KGA.

Table 5.1 compares the storage and computational cost.

5.2.2 ABE-based SE schemes

Attribute-based searchable encryption (ABSE) is a technique that enables secure search over encrypted data stored in the cloud [14]. In an ABSE scheme, the fine-grained access control is achieved with the help of an access policy/structure

Table 5.1 Comparative analysis of the existing schemes in literature

Scheme		Storage cost	Computational cost
PEKS based on *k*-Resilient IBE			
Khader [9]	Encrypted Index	$2\|G\| + \|\{0, 1\}^k\|$	$(3k + 5)E + 2H$
	Trapdoor	$6poly$	$6poly$
	Search		$4E + 1H$
PEKS using fuzzy function for keyword search trapdoor			
Xu et al. [11]	Encrypted Index	$2\|G\| + 2\|G_T\|$	$2P + 2E + 2E_T + 2H$
	Trapdoor	$2\|G\|$	$2H + 2E$
	Search		$1P + 1H$
Mamta et al. [13]	Encrypted Index	$2\|G\| + 4\|G_T\|$	$4P + 4E + 4E_T$
	Trapdoor	$2\|F_p\| + 2\|G\|$	$4E + 2H$
	Search		$1P + 1E_T$

which represents the relations among various attributes a user may possess. This access policy is either associated with the ciphertext or with the secret key of the user and thus results in two design frameworks and either one of them can be used as ABE. If the access policy is embedded in the ciphertext then it is called ciphertext-policy ABE (CP-ABE) [15, 16] and if it is associated with the secret key, then it is called key-policy ABE (KP-ABE) [6, 17].

In CP-ABE, the data owner has full control over his/her data because the access policy is associated with the ciphertext through which the data owner can define the users who can have access to his/her data. On the other hand, KP-ABE is suitable for scenarios where the data owner wants to broadcast his/her data. Here, only those users whose access policy agree with the attributes present in the broadcasted data will be able to gain access to the data. In both the frameworks, to provide fine-grained access control, there is a need of an extra entity called "attribute" which will decide who will access what. An attribute can be about anyone or anything. For example, *there is a Ph.D. scholar in the department of computer engineering.* Here, Ph.D. and computer engineering are the attributes of that user. If the institute has released marks of the computer engineering department, then a user who possess this attribute will be able to see his/her marks. Because of these attributes there will be an increase in same number of components in the ciphertext and the secret key of the user. Thus, there is an increase in complexity both in terms of storage cost and computational cost. Hence, it is required to develop secure and efficient ABSE schemes where this cost can be reduced by eliminating dependency on the attributes and making the size of ciphertext and secret key etc. constant. Many ABSE schemes have been proposed in the literature to support multi-user cloud storage environment [18, 19, 20]. The combination of ABE and SE definitely provides fine-grained search capabilities but it is achieved at the cost of increased complexity both in terms of storage cost and computational cost [21], [22].

Considering the page limit, we will provide highlights of some of KP-ABE- and CP-ABE based searchable encryption schemes.

5.2.2.1 VABKS

Zheng et al [21] developed the keyword search scheme using both KP-ABE and CP-ABE as the underlying encryption technique. They added the feature of verifiability of search results. Thus, Zheng et al. relaxed the honest assumption about the cloud server because now one can verify whether the cloud server has correctly executed the search algorithm or not. Their construction is based on a symmetric bilinear map where source and target groups are of prime order, p. They used a general access structure represented by the tree data structure and a top-down approach is used to get the shares of the secret value. Their scheme is secure against CKA in the selective security model under the decision linear assumption.

5.2.2.2 Attribute-based keyword search

Sun et al [23] proposed an attribute-based keyword search scheme for a multi-user setting with efficient user revocation. They used CP-ABE as the underlying encryption scheme. They claimed scalability in terms of search complexity which does not vary with the number of users. Their construction is based on a symmetric bilinear map where source and target groups are of prime order, p, and access structure consists of AND gate They have employed proxy re-encryption and lazy re-encryption techniques for efficient user revocation. Their scheme supports conjunctive keyword search, and is selectively secure against CKA under DBDH assumption.

5.2.2.3 A key-policy attribute-based temporary keyword search

Ameri et al. [24] proposed a temporary keyword search scheme to prevent information leakage from the search trapdoor. Their scheme is based on the key-policy design framework of the underlying ABE scheme. For the construction, they used a symmetric bilinear map, where source and target groups are of prime order, p. The access structure used in the scheme is of the general type represented by the tree data structure and a top-down approach is used to get the shares of the secret value. Their scheme is secure against CKA in a selective security model under a modified decisional Diffie–Hellman assumption. With respect to reducing computational cost, they made the number of pairing operations in the search algorithm independent of the number of time units specified in the search trapdoor.

5.2.2.4 Attribute-based searchable encryption for user level revocation

Mamta and Gupta [25] proposed an ABSE scheme with constant size user secret key and trapdoor. Further, the number of pairing operations in the search algorithm are constant. The constant term refers to the independence of these parameters from the number of attributes involved in the scheme. Thus, the resulting scheme reduces computational and storage cost and provides fast searching capabilities. Moreover, their scheme supports frequent changes in access policy. The access structure here is again of the general type and is represented by a tree data structure where internal represents AND, OR and threshold gate and the leaves represent the attributes. But unlike [24] they used a bottom-up approach to get the shares of a secret value. Their construction is based on a symmetric bilinear map where source and target groups are of prime order, p. Their scheme also handles the event of user revocation efficiently by delegating computationally intensive tasks to the cloud server. They proved security against CKA in the selective security model under the decision linear assumption.

5.2.2.5 Multi-authority attribute-based keyword search over encrypted cloud data

Miao et al [26] proposed a multi-authority attribute-based keyword search scheme, where independent attribute authorities can manage the attributes from a diverse domain very efficiently. They used the ciphertext-policy design framework of the ABE to build the keyword search scheme. The construction is based on a symmetric bilinear map where source and target groups are of prime order, p, and the access structure is represented by a monotone Boolean function. They used a linear secret sharing scheme (LSSS) to get the shares of a secret value. LSSS consists of a matrix of random elements and a mapping function which maps each row of the matrix with an attribute. Their scheme support attribute update and also provides tracing of malicious attribute authorities. Their scheme is selective secure under BDHE and DBDH assumption.

5.2.2.6 Searchable encryption for mobile healthcare networks

Mamta and Gupta [27] proposed a CP-ABE based searchable encryption scheme for the resource constrained mobile healthcare network. They made the size of both the ciphertext and the user secret key independent of the number of attributes involved in the scheme. Hence, their scheme is cost efficient. Moreover, their scheme results in fast search, as the number of pairing operations are also independent of the number of attributes. Their construction is based on an asymmetric bilinear map where source and target groups are of prime order, p, and the access structure is represented by AND gate. Their scheme is selective secure under augmented multi-sequence of exponents decisional Diffie–Hellman (aMSE-DDH) assumption.

5.2.2.7 Attribute-based searchable encryption for non-monotonic access structure

In an ABSE scheme, one assumption is made about the type of access structure supported by the scheme. Almost every ABSE scheme assumes a monotonic access structure. "Let $\mathcal{P} = \{P_1, P_2, ..., P_n\}$ be a set of parties or attributes. The collection $\mathbb{A} \subseteq 2^{\{P_1, P_2, ..., P_n\}} \setminus \Phi$ (non-empty subsets of $\mathcal{P}$) is monotonic if for any two arbitrary set of parties or attributes, i.e. B and C the following condition holds: $C \in \mathbb{A}$ iff $B \in \mathbb{A}$ and $B \subseteq C$," i.e. a monotonic access structure is a collection $\mathbb{A}$ of all non-empty subsets of $\mathcal{P}$ such that if a subset $B \in \mathbb{A}$ then all its superset should also belong to $\mathbb{A}$ [15]. For example, let $\mathcal{P} = \{1, 2, 3\}$ then the collection $\mathbb{A} = \{\{1, 2\}, \{2, 3\}, \{1, 2, 3\}\}$ is monotonic while the collection $\mathbb{A}' = \{\{1, 2\}, \{2, 3\}\}$ is non-monotonic.

For a better understanding, let's take one example in the form of the following Boolean formula: $A \vee (B \wedge C)$ is a monotonic access structure since $\{A, B\}$ as well as its superset $\{A, B, C\}$ satisfies the given formula. $A \vee (B \wedge C')$

is a non-monotonic access structure, since $\{A, B\}$ satisfies it but its superset $\{A, B, C\}$ does not satisfy the given formula. In other words, we can say that if a set and all its supersets satisfy the given access structure then that is known as monotonic access structure otherwise it is known as non-monotonic. From this example an important conclusion can be drawn that the presence of a NOT gate in an access structure makes it non-monotonic.

For the non-monotonic access structure several ABE schemes have been developed in the literature but none has been developed for ABSE schemes nor in a KP design framework. Thus, there exists an opportunity to provide support for a non-monotonic access structure in the case of an ABSE scheme so that one can include complicated access structures which can truly be represented by the Boolean formula to determine the searching capabilities. Mamta et al. [28]. introduced a CP-ABSE scheme that can handle non-monotonic access structure. They made use of a reduced ordered binary decision diagram to represent the access structure and achieved the non-monotonic property.

The notations used for the comparative analysis is given in Table 5.2.

A comparative analysis of the storage cost of ABSE schemes is given in Table 5.3. The storage cost is measured in terms of number and size (number of bits) of group elements involved in the outcome of each algorithm.

A comparative analysis of the computational cost of ABSE schemes is given in Table 5.4. The computational cost is measured in terms of number and different types of operations involved in each algorithm of the scheme.

From Table 5.3 and Table 5.4, it can be observed that the schemes [25], [27], and [28] have a constant storage cost and time complexity for the key-generation

Table 5.2 Description of the notation used in analysis of the similar ABE-based searchable encryption schemes in literature

Notation	Description
$\|G\|, \|G_T\|$	Length of source (G) and target group (G_T) elements respectively in case of symmetric bilinear pairing
$\|G_1\|, \|G_2\|, \|G_T\|$	Length of source (G_1, G_2) and target group (G_T) elements respectively in case of asymmetric bilinear pairing
$\|Z_p\|$	Length of an element of a group of integers of prime order, p
P	Bilinear pairing operation
E, E_T	Exponent operation in source and target group respectively
H	Collision resistant one-way hash function
ξ	# of attributes associated with users
N	# of attributes associated with access policy
U	# of authorized users in the system
t	# of time units for which a trapdoor is valid
k	# of keywords in case of a multi-keyword search scheme
T	# of valid paths

Table 5.3 Storage cost analysis of the attribute-based searchable encryption schemes

Scheme	Secret key size	Ciphertext size	Trapdoor size
Zheng et al. [21]	$(2N)\|G\|$ $(2\xi+1)\|G\|$	$(\xi+3)\|G\|$ $(2N+3)\|G\|$	$(2N+2)\|G\|$ $(2\xi+3)\|G\|$
Sun et al. [23]	$1\|Z_p\|+(2\xi+1)\|G\|$	$(N+2)\|G\|$	$(2\xi+2)\|G\|$
Ameri et al. [24]	$(2N)\|G\|$	$(\xi+3)\|G\|+1Z_p$	$(2N+t+1)\|G\|$
Mamta & B.B. Gupta [25]	$1\|Z_p\|+3\|G\|$	$(\xi+3+2U)\|G\|$	$6\|G\|$
Miao et al. [26]	$(3\xi+4)\|G\|+3\|Z_p\|$	$(3N+3)\|G\|+2\|G_T\|+N\|Z_p\|$	$2\|G\|+1\|Z_p\|$
Mamta & B.B. Gupta [27]	$2\|G_1\|$	$1\|G_1\|+2\|G_2\|+1\|G_T\|$	$\|G_1\|+(\xi+1)\|G_2\|$
Mamta et al. [28]	$2\|G\|$	$(T+1)\|G\|+2\|G_T\|$	$2\|G\|+1\|Z_p\|$

Table 5.4 Computational cost analysis of the attribute-based searchable encryption schemes

Scheme	Key generation	Encryption	Trapdoor generation	Search
Zheng et al. [21]	$3NE+NH$ $(2\xi+1)\|G\|$	$(\xi+4)E+\xi H$	$(2N+2)E$	$(2\xi+2)P+\xi E_T$
Sun et al. [22]	$(2\xi+2)E$	$(3N+2)E+1H$	$(2\xi+1)E+2H$	$(N+1)P+NE_T$
Ameri et al. [24]	$(2N+1)E+NH$	$(\xi+4)E+(\xi+2)H$	$(2N+t+1)E+$ $(t+1)H$	$(2\xi+2)P+\xi E_T+tE$
Mamta and Gupta [25]	$3E+1H$	$(\xi+6)E+(k+1)H$	$7E+1P+1H$	$(\xi+2)E+6P$
Miao et al. [26]	$(3\xi+8)E$	$(4N+3)E+2E_T+P$	$(2\xi+2)E$	$2P$
Mamta and Gupta [27]	$2E$	$(2N+1)E+2E_T+1H+1P$	$(\xi+3)E+1H$	$4P+1E_T$
Mamta et al. [28]	$2E$	$(T+1)E+1H+2E_T$	$2E+1H$	$(T+1)P+1E_T$

algorithm in terms of the number of attributes involved, as compared to the other schemes. For the encryption algorithm, each of the given schemes has variable storage as well as computational cost except in [27] where the storage cost is again constant. For the trapdoor-generation algorithms, again in [25], [27], and [28] the storage cost is constant while [25] and [28] were able to make the computational cost invariant to the number of attributes. In the *Search* algorithm, it can be observed that [26] and [27] were able to make the constant number of pairing operations and thereby achieved fast search.

5.3 CHAPTER SUMMARY

In a multi-user cloud environment, public-key setting is a preferable choice to develop the searchable encryption scheme as the symmetric-key schemes suffer from the complicated process of secret key sharing. This chapter explained in detail the concept of searchable encryption in a public-key setting. It provided the general structure of the searchable encryption scheme in asymmetric key setting. Further, this chapter mainly discussed the searchable encryption techniques developed using IBE and ABE. Between them, we have identified ABE as a suitable choice because it provides fine-grained access control capabilities which makes it an appropriate scheme that can truly handle multiple users in an efficient manner. Further, we have performed a comparative analysis of existing schemes in literature in this setting.

REFERENCES

1. Z. Wang, J. Ye, and J. Wang, "An efficient traceable data sharing scheme in cloud computing for mobile devices," *Int. J. High Perform. Comput. Netw*, vol. 12, no. 2, pp. 156–165, 2018.
2. S.-H. Heng, and K. Kurosawa, "k-resilient identity-based encryption in the standard model," in *Cryptographers' Track at the RSA Conference*, 2004, pp. 67–80.
3. J. Wang, and C. Wang, "Full secure identity-based encryption scheme over lattices for wireless sensor networks in the standard model," *Int. J. High Perform. Comput. Netw*, vol. 12, no. 2, pp. 111–117, 2018.
4. Y. Lu, G. Wang, J. Li, and J. Shen, "Efficient designated server identity-based encryption with conjunctive keyword search," *Ann. Telecommun*, vol. 72, no. 5–6, pp. 359–370, 2017.
5. Y. Miao, J. Ma, F. Wei, K. Zhang, and Z. Liu, "VKSE-DO: Verifiable keyword search over encrypted data for dynamic data-owner," *Int. J. High Perform. Comput. Netw*, vol. 12, no. 1, pp. 39–48, 2018.
6. J. Zhang, and H. Gao, "A compact construction for non-monotonic key-policy attribute-based encryption," *Int. J. High Perform. Comput. Netw*, vol. 13, no. 3, pp. 321–330, 2019.
7. S. Zhu, and Y. Han, "Secure data outsourcing scheme in cloud computing with attribute-based encryption," *Int. J. High Perform. Comput. Netw*, vol. 12, no. 2, pp. 128–136, 2018.
8. D. Boneh, G. Di Crescenzo, R. Ostrovsky, and G. Persiano, "Public key encryption with keyword search," in *International Conference on the Theory and Applications of Cryptographic Techniques*, 2004, pp. 506–522.
9. D. Khader, "Public key encryption with keyword search based on k-resilient IBE," in *International Conference on Computational Science and Its Applications*, 2007, pp. 1086–1095.
10. M. Abdalla *et al.*, "Searchable encryption revisited: Consistency properties, relation to anonymous IBE, and extensions," *J. Cryptol.*, vol. 21, no. 3, pp. 350–391, 2008.

11. P. Xu, H. Jin, Q. Wu, and W. Wang, "Public-key encryption with fuzzy keyword search: A provably secure scheme under keyword guessing attack," *IEEE Trans. Comput*, vol. 62, no. 11, pp. 2266–2277, 2012.

12. D. Boneh, and M. Franklin, "Identity-based encryption from the Weil pairing," in *Annual International Cryptology Conference*, 2001, pp. 213–229.

13. Mamta, B. B. Gupta, and S. T. Ali, "ISEkFT: An IBE-based searchable encryption scheme with k-keyword fuzzy search trapdoor," *J. Inf. Technol. Res*, vol. 12, no. 3, pp. 133–153, 2019.

14. M. Sookhak, F. R. Yu, M. K. Khan, Y. Xiang, and R. Buyya, "Attribute-based data access control in mobile cloud computing: Taxonomy and open issues," *Futur. Gener. Comput. Syst*, vol. 72, pp. 273–287, 2017.

15. J. Bethencourt, A. Sahai, and B. Waters, "Ciphertext-policy attribute-based encryption," in *2007 IEEE Symposium on Security and Privacy (SP'07)*, 2007, pp. 321–334.

16. X. Yang, and W. Ding, "Researches on data encryption scheme based on CP-ASBE of cloud storage," *Int. J. High Perform. Comput. Netw*, vol. 14, no. 2, pp. 219–228, 2019.

17. V. Goyal, O. Pandey, A. Sahai, and B. Waters, "Attribute-based encryption for fine-grained access control of encrypted data," in *Proceedings of the 13th ACM Conference on Computer and Communications Security*, 2006, pp. 89–98.

18. L. Ibraimi, Q. Tang, P. Hartel, and W. Jonker, "Efficient and Provable Secure Ciphertext-Policy Attribute-Based Encryption Schemes," in *International Conference on Information Security Practice and Experience*, 2009, pp. 1–12.

19. G. Wang, Q. Liu, J. Wu, and M. Guo, "Hierarchical attribute-based encryption and scalable user revocation for sharing data in cloud servers," *Comput. Secur*, vol. 30, no. 5, pp. 320–331, 2011.

20. C. Chen, Z. Zhang, and D. Feng, "Efficient ciphertext policy attribute-based encryption with constant-size ciphertext and constant computation-cost," in *International Conference on Provable Security*, 2011, pp. 84–101.

21. Q. Zheng, S. Xu, and G. Ateniese, "VABKS: Verifiable attribute-based keyword search over outsourced encrypted data," *in Infocom, 2014 proceedings IEEE*, 2014, pp. 522–530.

22. W. Sun, S. Yu, W. Lou, Y. T. Hou, and H. Li, "Protecting your right: Verifiable attribute-based keyword search with fine-grained owner-enforced search authorization in the cloud," *IEEE Trans. Parallel Distrib. Syst*, vol. 27, no. 4, pp. 1187–1198, 2016.

23. W. Sun, S. Yu, W. Lou, Y. T. Hou, and H. Li, "Protecting your right: Attribute-based keyword search with fine-grained owner-enforced search authorization in the cloud," in *IEEE INFOCOM 2014-IEEE Conference on Computer Communications*, 2014, pp. 226–234.

24. M. H. Ameri, M. Delavar, J. Mohajeri, and M. Salmasizadeh, "A key-policy attribute-based temporary keyword search scheme for secure cloud storage," *IEEE Trans. Cloud Comput.*, 2018.

25. Mamta, and B. B. Gupta,, "An efficient KP design framework of attribute-based searchable encryption for user level revocation in cloud," *Concurr. Comput. Pract. Exp.*, https://doi.org/10.1002/cpe.5291

26. Y. Miao, R. Deng, X. Liu, K.-K. R. Choo, H. Wu, and H. Li, "Multi-authority attribute-based keyword search over encrypted cloud data," *IEEE Trans. Dependable Secur. Comput.*, 2019.

27. Mamta, and B. B. Gupta, "An attribute-based keyword search for m-health networks," *J. Comput. Virol. Hacking Tech.*, pp. 1–16, 2020.
28. Mamta, and B. B. Gupta, "An attribute-based searchable encryption Scheme for Non-monotonic access structure," in *Handbook of Research on Intrusion Detection Systems*, IGI Global, 2020, pp. 263–283.

Chapter 6

Design and development tools and inter-domain application

THE DESIGN AND DEVELOPMENT of searchable encryption schemes essentially requires a knowledge of mathematics, but once developed and proved secure, we need to implement it to check the practically. In this chapter, we will discuss the choice of language to implement these schemes, available libraries, and the different data sets available for testing. Further, we will discuss some applications of searchable encryption in several areas other than cryptography.

6.1 LANGUAGE AND LIBRARY OPTIONS

A searchable encryption scheme is a collection of different algorithms working together to achieve a common goal of searching encrypted data. Therefore, any language in which the user is comfortable can be used for implementation purposes. In the public-key setting, pairing operations are performed for which pairing libraries have to be used. Therefore, it is suggested to use the same language as the pairing library for better compatibility.

6.1.1 Toolkits for symmetric searchable encryption schemes

For the searchable encryption schemes in the symmetric-key setting the following toolkits are available to evaluate the searchable encryption.

OpenSSE's Cryptographic Toolkit: This toolkit has a cryptographic layer which provides interfaces and implementations of features like pseudo-random functions, hash functions, and encryption schemes, on which a typical searchable encryption scheme relies. This toolkit contains single keyword search schemes implemented in C and C++. It offers the required level of abstraction to easily implement searchable encryption schemes. The famous cryptography libraries like OpenSSL do not provide interfaces for the building blocks of searchable encryption schemes. However, it is still a research project and is suggested not to be used for sensitive information.

The Clusion Library: Clusion is another software library that is worth mentioning if we are talking about symmetric searchable encryption (SSE). Not only does it provide a modular implementation of recent SSE schemes, but also all the implementations have sub-linear asymptotic search complexity while considering the worst case. Further, it gives constructions that support disjunction, conjunction operations in case of multi-keyword search and also supports the trivial single keyword search.

6.1.2 Pairing libraries for searchable encryption in a public-key setting

The searchable encryption schemes in the public-key setting are developed mainly using identity-based encryption, attribute-based encryption, and predicate encryption, etc. and these advanced encryption schemes typically use the pairing concept in their construction. There are several pairing libraries available, and some of the popular libraries among them are described as follows:

PBC (Pairing-Based Cryptography) Library: This is a free C library for performing the pairing operation. It is developed on the GMP library, which performs mathematical operations. The PBC library is an integral part of the pairing-based cryptosystem [1]. Because it uses the GMP library underneath, the pairing times are very short, although it is written in C. Thus, speed and portability are among its prime features. Further, essential functions such as elliptic-curve arithmetic and pairing computations could be easily performed. Boneh-Lynn-Shacham short signatures [2], Hess identity-based signatures [3] and Paterson identity-based signatures [4] are examples of some of the cryptosystems tested using this library.

JPBC (Java Pairing-Based Cryptography) Library: As the name suggests, the Java Pairing-Based Cryptographic library is based on the Java language [5]. It is an extension of the PBC library given by Lynn [1]. JPBC-based implementation supports multithreading and employs memory-mapped files to optimize primary memory usage. JPBC uses a wrapper to delegate the pairing computations to the PBC library. In addition to the bilinear maps, JPBC also provides support for multi-linear maps. Several functional encryption schemes and signature schemes have been successfully tested using the JPBC library.

Charm: Charm is a python-based library. Prototypes of advanced cryptosystems could be quickly and seamlessly created using the Charm framework [6]. Code reuse, readability, and simplicity are some of the striking features of Charm. It provides support for various mathematical settings, including integer rings/fields, bilinear and non-bilinear elliptic-curve groups. It has a base crypto library, which includes symmetric encryption schemes, hash functions and pseudorandom number generators.

Further, Charm provides standard application programming interfaces to construct digital signatures and encryption schemes. Moreover, it gives a "protocol engine" to simplify the process of implementing multi-party protocols. An integrated compiler for interactive and non-interactive zero-knowledge proofs is also provided by the Charm framework. Thus, it is the most comprehensive framework as per the functionalities it offers.

Multiprecision integer and rational arithmetic cryptographic library: The multiprecision integer and rational arithmetic cryptographic library (MIRACL) is a C language-based software library [7]. It is one of the preferred open-source software development toolkits for elliptic-curve cryptography. The feature which makes MIRACL different from any other cryptographic library is its commitment to provide the security solution to resource constrained environments like mobile applications, embedded systems, etc. Many renowned organizations around the globe, including Panasonic, Hitachi, Toyota, Intel, and many more, have used the services of MIRACL. Another important feature of MIRACL is its support for state-of-the-art security technologies, including searchable encryption.

RELIC: RELIC is another example of a cryptographic toolkit. Efficiency, flexibility, and portability are its main features [8]. Various algorithms are implemented using RELIC. Among them, some are elliptic curves over prime and binary fields, bilinear maps and related extension fields. Several cryptographic protocols like RSA, Rabin, and Boneh-Boyen short signatures [9] systems are also implemented using RELIC.

6.2 DATA SETS

There are different datasets available to conduct the simulations and evaluate the time complexity of the algorithms involved in the searchable encryption scheme.

Enron email dataset: The Enron email dataset carries approximately 500,000 emails generated by employees of the Enron organization [10]. It was acquired by the Federal Energy Regulatory commission throughout its research of Enron's collapse. This dataset was gathered and organized under the Cognitive Assistant that Learns and Organizes (CALO) project. It carries statistics from approximately 150 users, in most cases senior management of Enron. The data is organized into folders. These records were made public and published to the Internet by the Federal Energy Regulatory Commission in the course of its research. Later this dataset was purchased by Leslie Kaelbling at MIT, who identified a number of integrity problems which were then corrected and the data set made available for research projects. The invalid email addresses were transformed to a general form like user@enron.com (when the recipient was specified) or to no_address@enron.com when no recipient was specified.

Internet request for comments (RFC): This dataset has 6,870 plaintext files with a total size about 349MB [11]. To extract the keywords from each RFC file, a hermetic word frequency counter [12] is generally used.

6.3 INTER-DOMAIN APPLICATIONS

Searchable encryption is not just restricted to the cryptography domain but can be applied to and combined with different platforms. Apart from the application of searchable encryption on the cloud platform there are other application scenarios that have been seen in the literature. Researchers have applied and tested this concept for different platforms like IoT (Internet of things), wireless sensor networks (WSN), fog computing and the combination of these [13, 14, 15]. Most recently, blockchain technology has been leveraged to build more robust searchable encryption schemes. Most of the developments in this direction has been seen from 2017 onwards.

A new area where searchable encryption application has been seen is the cloud-assisted wireless sensor networks (CWSN). Xu [16] proposed a lightweight searchable encryption scheme for CWSN with a reduced cost of generating ciphertext and performing search. The owner of the sensor network generates public and secret key pairs and stores the public components at all the sensor nodes. The sensor nodes collect and store the encrypted data on the cloud server. To retrieve the data, the data owner generates a trapdoor for the keyword and sends it to the cloud server to perform the search.

IoT devices contribute the majority of data in today's digital world and the collected data is stored in cloud servers. The collected data may be sensitive; therefore, searchable encryption can have applications for cloud-based IoT. Wu et al. [17] proposed a searchable encryption scheme for the same. The working of their system is the same as the standard searchable encryption in a public-key setting. Apart from the basic functionality, they focused on developing the KGA resistant scheme.

Miao et al. [18] applied fine-grained conjunctive keyword search to fog computing. It is basically an extension of cloud computing where fog nodes are placed between the end users and the cloud. Their scheme is lightweight in the sense that most of the computationally intensive tasks are delegated to the fog nodes. The end users only perform the partial computations; the final ciphertext and even the final trapdoor are generated by the fog nodes and sent to the cloud server. The fog nodes receive the search result returned by the cloud server and perform partial decryption to further reduce the burden on end users. The cloud server has the role of searching like always and instead of returning the search result to the end user, now it returns it to the intermediate fog nodes that perform all necessary computations. They also take into account the process of updating the attributes in the access policy, hence supporting dynamic policy. The data from end users are collected by the IoT devices (wearable or mobile devices) used by these users.

During this timeframe, when research was going on to test the applicability of searchable encryption in different scenarios as discussed above, there came a major milestone in the journey of searchable encryption schemes. This milestone was achieved by using the most innovative technology of the century: blockchain technology. We have seen a huge revolution initiated by this technology in different sectors such as finance, healthcare, voting and a lot more. Hu et al. [19] proposed an entirely new platform for the searchable encryption. They leveraged the power of smart contracts to develop a secure searchable encryption in a symmetric-key setting. The resulting scheme was quite robust as we now need not worry about situations like a malicious cloud server or whether the cloud server is dishonest. The inherent design of the blockchain technology take cares of these issues. Instead of using the cloud server, the data owner stores his/her data in an encrypted form over the public blockchain platform, Ethereum. The scheme was implemented and tested to check the applicability in practical scenarios. Most recently in June, 2020, the application of blockchain technology has been seen in developing searchable encryption in a public-key setting by Liu et al. [17]. They have not replaced the cloud server with the blockchain, but have leveraged blockchain technology to reduce computational burden and to build more realistic SE schemes. They have used consortium blockchain to initialize the system, generate the final trapdoor and handle the event of user revocation. The cloud as usual stores the encrypted data and performs partial decryption on the behalf of users. The blockchain technology here makes the SE scheme decentralized by completely eliminating the need of a central authority and has also reduced the computational burden from data users.

6.4 CHAPTER SUMMARY

This chapter discussed different open-source tools for the design and development of secure, searchable encryption schemes. It also outlined some of the best practices and guidelines for ensuring the security of searchable encryption schemes. Further, this chapter discussed different areas of application for searchable encryption and how this technique plays an important role in different domains.

REFERENCES

1. B. Lynn, "PBC library," https://crypto.stanford.edu/pbc/, 2006.
2. D. Boneh, B. Lynn, and H. Shacham, "Short signatures from the Weil pairing," in *International Conference on the Theory and Application of Cryptology and Information Security*, 2001, pp. 514–532.

3. F. Hess, "Efficient identity based signature schemes based on pairings," in *International Workshop on Selected Areas in Cryptography*, 2002, pp. 310–324.

4. K. G. Paterson, "ID-based signatures from pairings on elliptic curves," *Electron. Lett*, vol. 38, no. 18, pp. 1025–1026, 2002.

5. A. De Caro, and V. Iovino, "jPBC: Java pairing based cryptography," in *2011 IEEE Symposium on Computers and Communications (ISCC)*, 2011, pp. 850–855.

6. J. A. Akinyele *et al.*, "Charm: A framework for rapidly prototyping cryptosystems," *J. Cryptogr. Eng.*, vol. 3, no. 2, pp. 111–128, 2013.

7. M. Scott, "MIRACL-A multiprecision integer and rational arithmetic C/C++ library," http//www.shamus.ie, 2003.

8. D. F. Aranha, "RELIC is an efficient library for cryptography." http://code.google.com/p/relic-toolkit/, 2013.

9. D. Boneh, X. Boyen, and H. Shacham, "Short group signatures," in *Annual International Cryptology Conference*, 2004, pp. 41–55.

10. W. W. Cohen, "Enron email dataset webpage." Carnegie Mellon University, http://www.cs.cmu.edu/~enron, 2009

11. "RFC: Request for comments database," https://www.ietf.org/rfc/

12. "HERMETIC: Hermetic word frequency counter," http://www.hermetic.ch/wfc/wfc.htm

13. A. Tewari, and B. B. Gupta, "Cryptanalysis of a novel ultra-lightweight mutual authentication protocol for IoT devices using RFID tags," *The Journal of Supercomputing*, vol. 73, no. 3, pp. 1085–1102, 2017.

14. B. B. Gupta, and D. P. Agrawal, eds. *Handbook of Research on Cloud Computing and Big Data Applications in IoT*. IGI Global, 2019.

15. B. B. Gupta, ed. *Computer and Cyber Security: Principles, Algorithm, Applications, and Perspectives*. CRC Press, 2018.

16. P. Xu, S. He, W. Wang, W. Susilo, and H. Jin, "Lightweight searchable public-key encryption for cloud-assisted wireless sensor networks," *IEEE Trans. Ind. Informatics*, vol. 14, no. 8, pp. 3712–3723, 2017.

17. L. Wu, B. Chen, K.-K. R. Choo, and D. He, "Efficient and secure searchable encryption protocol for cloud-based internet of things," *J. Parallel Distrib. Comput*, vol. 111, pp. 152–161, 2018.

18. Y. Miao, J. Ma, X. Liu, J. Weng, H. Li, and H. Li, "Lightweight fine-grained search over encrypted data in fog computing," *IEEE Trans. Serv. Comput.*, 2018.

19. S. Hu, C. Cai, Q. Wang, C. Wang, X. Luo, and K. Ren, "Searching an Encrypted Cloud Meets Blockchain: A Decentralized, Reliable and Fair Realization," in *IEEE INFOCOM 2018-IEEE Conference on Computer Communications*, 2018, pp. 792–800.

20. S. Liu, J. Yu, Y. Xiao, Z. Wan, S. Wang, and B. Yan, "BC-SABE: Blockchain-aided searchable attribute-based encryption for Cloud-IoT," *IEEE Internet Things J.*, 2020.

Chapter 7

Searchable encryption applications, challenges and future research directions

SEARCHABLE ENCRYPTION APPLICATIONS AND FUTURE RESEARCH DIRECTIONS are the main highlights of this chapter. In addition, we will discuss the critical research challenges encountered while designing searchable encryption schemes.

7.1 SEARCHABLE ENCRYPTION APPLICATIONS

Cloud-based storage allows multiple data owners to share their data with multiple users. Public-key setting is the suitable choice to support such a scenario. Therefore, to efficiently use cloud-based storage, we aim to utilize public-key cryptographic primitives to provide confidentiality of the data. Further, the number of users as well as the amount of data stored over cloud-based storage is increasing rapidly. Therefore, to retrieve valuable information, there is a need to develop an efficient searchable encryption scheme [1].

> *General application of searchable encryption:* Searchable encryption schemes have numerous applications in areas where we want both security of the data and accessibility to the data. For example, in a banking system, confidentiality of the customer's data is important but at the same time the bank wants the data to be processed by designated employees to provide various services to its customers. The confidentiality part can be achieved by applying encryption. However, the data a banking system deals with may be huge, hence there is a need of an encryption technique through which one can perform search without actually downloading and decrypting the data. Similar to the banking system, there is a large class of applications where searchable encryption can make a difference. Further, searchable encryption has applications in multiple domains like secure auditing of network and financial logs, privacy of health monitoring systems, remote data storage which are untrusted in nature and so on.
>
> *Application of public-key encryption with keyword search (PEKS) and its extensions:* The application of PEKS in secure email retrieval proposed by Boneh et al. [2] has been seen in the literature. Later Tang and Chen [3]

93

proposed an extension of PEKS that has application in the detection of junk emails.

Application of attribute-based searchable encryption: Searchable encryption schemes developed using ABE provide fine-grained search capabilities to their users and have applications in the field of healthcare networks. The data owner (patient) can store his/her health data online in an encrypted form to provide differential access to different users like researchers, doctors or insurance agents. Since all the users belong to entirely different domains it is not possible for a single authority to manage such diverse domains. Hence, there is a need to devise a multi-authority approach such that each authority independently manages the attributes of their domain.

7.2 RESEARCH CHALLENGES

There are three main research challenges in developing a searchable encryption scheme: *i*) security, *ii*) efficiency and *iii*) query expressiveness [4]. The security of a searchable encryption scheme is measured in terms of how well the scheme hides both the data file and the associated keywords. It is assumed that the scheme is more secure if the adversary is more powerful. The power of an adversary is measured in terms of facilities provided to him/her, such as access to oracles and the type of queries he/she can ask. Moreover, if weaker security assumptions are used in the security proof of a searchable encryption scheme, the resulting technique is assumed to be more secure. The time cost of breaking the weak assumption is much greater than the strong assumption, thus making strong assumptions relatively risker. The weaker assumptions are also known as standard assumptions.

The efficiency of a searchable encryption scheme is measured in terms of computational, storage and communication costs [5, 6, 7]. The computational cost is measured in terms of the number of operations and the type of operations required to generate the ciphertext, search trapdoor and finally to perform search. Similarly, the storage cost is measured in terms of memory space required to store the ciphertext, search trapdoor, public parameters and the secret key. The communication cost is measured in terms of the amount of time required to send the secret key, search trapdoor and the search result to the intended recipient. A searchable encryption scheme is assumed to be efficient if the associated costs are reduced to minimum. The query expressiveness of a searchable encryption scheme is measured in terms of the variety of search queries supported by the scheme. Expressiveness of queries may vary from the simplest equality query to multidimensional range queries.

There exists a tradeoff between these three parameters; a more secure scheme may be less efficient and vice-versa. Similarly, a scheme which supports more expressive search queries may be less secure and may be less efficient.

7.3 DIRECTIONS FOR FUTURE WORK

Basically, searching is a very fundamental operation and we have seen how efficiently the search engines work on plain data. The research community wants the same flexibility and natural feeling while searching on encrypted data stored at shared cloud storage. Therefore, a lot of research is going specially in the field of public-key-based searchable encryption because the public-key setting is a preferable choice for the shared cloud storage environment. Some of the future research directions in this domain are highlighted in Figure 7.1.

Searchable encryption be applied in any domain where confidentiality of the data is required and without compromising data privacy. We want a third

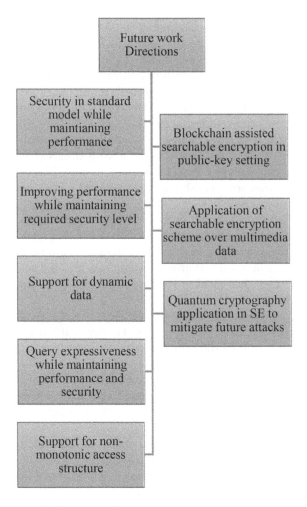

Figure 7.1 Directions for future work.

party to retrieve the required data in such a way that the third party will not get any information about what is being searched. The existing public-key-based searchable encryption schemes try to accommodate the maximum possible features but there still exists some scope for improvement because none of them is complete in every sense. Therefore, depending upon the application one should decide the functionalities that should be present in the searchable encryption scheme under consideration. However, there are some useful functionalities which, if added, can significantly improve the usability of the searchable encryption scheme and these are as follows:

- To make the searchable encryption scheme more natural it should support expressive search queries that can be represented by any Boolean formula.
- Most of the searchable encryption schemes in the literature are proved secure in the random oracle model (ROM). ROM definitely makes the construction easy but it assumes idealistic conditions. Therefore, to prove the security one should consider the standard model which results in a scheme that can work well in real-life situations.
- More emphasis should be given towards developing fully secure searchable encryption systems. Most of the searchable encryption schemes in the literature offer selective security.
- In the practical scenario, when someone stores his/her data to the cloud server with the intention of sharing it with others then he/she should also take care that their data is always up to date. Therefore, the searchable encryption schemes should be developed with a provision to support dynamic data.
- The verifiability of search results returned by the cloud server is a key feature that can add more security to the searchable encryption schemes. Most of the existing schemes in the literature assume the cloud server to be honest in a sense that it correctly executes the search algorithm. However, there is a need to relax this assumption to make the scheme more secure.
- The current searchable encryption schemes perform search for the complete keyword given in the trapdoor. However, if our requirement is to search only a part of the keyword with the same trapdoor, there is a lot of scope to work in this domain.
- Attribute-based searchable encryption (ABSE) schemes are becoming popular due to their fine-grained searching feature. However, in most of the ABSE schemes the storage and computation cost varies linearly with the attributes. This significantly reduces performance and scalability. Therefore, efforts should be made to make the associated costs independent of the number of attributes involved.
- With ABSE one common assumption is made about the access structures. They are assumed to be monotonic and therefore do not support negative attributes. To make the access structure expressive, we should

be able to represent it in the form of any Boolean formula. This has been completely neglected in the case of searchable encryption schemes and efforts are required to work in this direction.

- Searchable encryption has been integrated with recent technologies like blockchain technology to provide a more robust and realistic platform [8, 9, 10]. The evidence of this integration has been seen in the literature in case of symmetric-key setting. However, this integration is yet to be explored in the public-key setting.

- The application of searchable encryption in public-key and symmetric-key settings has been seen only on text data. However, in today's digital world it is not only text that we want to securely store and share, it can be any multimedia data like an image, video etc. None of the existing schemes has been tested for such data. Therefore, this direction can also be explored to test the feasibility of existing schemes for different kinds of data.

- Finally, to resist the quantum attacks which are the potential threats to our current cryptographic algorithms, there is need to introduce the quantum cryptography while developing the searchable encryption schemes to ensure security in the future [11, 12].

There have been tremendous developments in the area of searching over plain data. However, when the encrypted data is considered, the current search functionalities are very limited and do not provide the same seamless experience that we get in the case of plain data. Hence, there is a lot of scope in building such schemes which can efficiently perform search over encrypted data as well as support complex search queries.

7.4 CHAPTER SUMMARY

This chapter highlighted the open challenges associated with searchable encryption and provided insights into future research directions in the field. From our in-depth study of searchable encryption techniques, it can be remarked that searchable encryption is not just a concept related to cryptography, but it is a commodity that can have applicability in our real life in sectors such as banking, health care, auditing and many more where the aim is to ensure confidentiality and accessibility at the same time.

REFERENCES

1. R. Bharathi, and R. Selvarani, "Software reliability assessment of safety critical system using computational intelligence," *International Journal of Software Science and Computational Intelligence (IJSSCI)*, vol. 11, no. 3, p. 1–25, 2019.
2. D. Boneh, G. Di Crescenzo, R. Ostrovsky, and G. Persiano, "Public key encryption with keyword search," in *International Conference on the Theory and Applications of Cryptographic Techniques*, 2004, pp. 506–522.

3. Q. Tang, and L. Chen, "Public-key encryption with registered keyword search," in *European Public Key Infrastructure Workshop*, 2009, pp. 163–178.
4. C. Bösch, P. Hartel, W. Jonker, and A. Peter, "A survey of provably secure searchable encryption," *ACM Comput. Surv*, vol. 47, no. 2, p. 1–51, 2014.
5. J. Ye, M. Miao, P. Chen, and X. Chen, "Comparable encryption scheme supporting multiple users in cloud computing," *Int. J. High Perform. Comput. Netw*, vol. 11, no. 1, p. 24–33, 2018.
6. L. Zhang, Z. Wang, Y. Mu, and Y. Hu, "Fully secure hierarchical inner product encryption for privacy preserving keyword searching in cloud," *Int. J. High Perform. Comput. Netw*, vol. 11, no. 1, p. 45–54, 2018.
7. J. Yang, L. Wang, and J. Baek, "A privacy preserving and fine-grained access control scheme in DaaS based on efficient DSP re-encryption," *Int. J. High Perform. Comput. Netw*, vol. 11, no. 3, p. 231–241, 2018.
8. S. Tanwar, K. Parekh, and R. Evans, "Blockchain-based electronic healthcare record system for healthcare 4.0 applications," *J. Inf. Secur. Appl*, vol. 50, https://doi.org/10.1016/j.jisa.2019.102407, 2020.
9. Q. Tang, "Towards blockchain-enabled searchable encryption," in *International Conference on Information and Communications Security*, 2019, pp. 482–500.
10. S. Liu, J. Yu, Y. Xiao, Z. Wan, S. Wang, and B. Yan, "BC-SABE: Blockchain-aided searchable attribute-based encryption for Cloud-IoT," *IEEE Internet Things J.*, https://doi.org/10.1109/JIOT.2020.2993231, 2020.
11. A. P. Pljonkin, "Vulnerability of the synchronization process in the quantum key distribution system," *International Journal of Cloud Applications and Computing (IJCAC)*, vol. 9, no. 1, p. 50–58, 2019.
12. A. A. Abd El-Latif, B. Abd-El-Atty, M. S. Hossain, M. A. Rahman, A. Alamri, and B. B. Gupta, "Efficient quantum information hiding for remote medical image sharing," *IEEE Access*, vol. 6, p. 21075–21083, 2018.

Index